POWERHOUSE STATE OF MIND

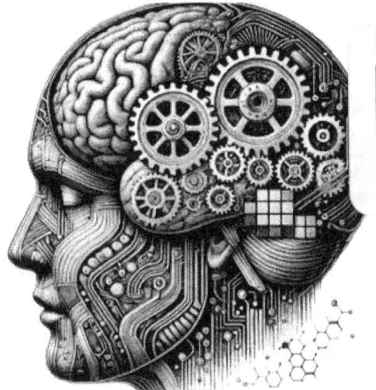

Confidence Keys to Elevate, Expand, and Embody Executive Presence

Kristie Kennedy

Acknowledgements

We are thrilled to bring you Powerhouse State of Mind: Confidence Keys to Elevate, Expand, and Enhance Executive Presence by Kristie Kennedy. With its powerful title, this book is a guide to unlocking your inner strength and leadership potential. It offers actionable insights and a fresh perspective from Kristie Kennedy, an executive leadership coach and motivational speaker, on leading with confidence and resilience.

Kristie's wisdom, rooted in her extensive experience as an executive leadership coach and motivational speaker, shines through every chapter. Whether you are a seasoned leader or just beginning your journey, this book equips you with practical tools to elevate your presence, expand your influence, and overcome obstacles with grace and determination. It is a powerful resource that will leave you feeling empowered and ready to take on any challenge.

Rapid Publishers
Book Cover Designer

Powerhouse State of Mind is bursting with seeds of inspirational ideas that will live beyond the pages of Kristie's imagination. As an avid reader, the message within this literary work captivates the spirit and will liberate dormant potential.

As a creative thought partner working alongside Kristie, she understands the power of utilizing words to provoke the procrastinator to take audacious action, to teach the fearful how to wield the sword of courage and to incite the introverted leader with confidence keys to emerge from obscurity and boldly use their voice freely in any setting. Crafting an interactive learning tool that could undeniably facilitate personal growth was our top priority.

Nauman Akbar @Naumanakbar269
Interior Book Designer

Copyright © 2024 by Kristie Kennedy.

All rights reserved.

Printed in the United States of America. Except as permitted under the United States Copyright Act of 1976, no part of this publication may be reproduced or distributed in any form or by any means, or stored in database or retrieval system, without the prior written permission of the publisher.

All Rights Reserved

ISBN: 978-0-9758954-3-6

Foreword

We rarely encounter someone who is not only a covenant friend but a beacon of inspiration, strength, and exemplary leadership in every facet of life. For over 25 years, Kristie Kennedy has been a never-ending source of encouragement, unwavering support, and a true testament to what it means to live audaciously. Over the years, our friendship has encompassed joy, mutual respect, and that "iron sharpening iron" type of growth and accountability. We have shared tears and laughter, countless testimonies of triumph, and challenges that pierced the depths of our existence. Through it all, Kristie's tenacity, and indomitable belief in the power of transformation have remained steadfast.

Kristie's unique blend of leadership insights and compassionate understanding of our challenges sets her apart. She is not just deeply invested in her growth but equally passionate about helping others rise to their highest potential. This spirit of dedication and empowerment is evident in her work as an executive leadership coach, speaker, author, and image confidence expert. With over 20 years of speaking experience, she has graced stages like TEDx and inspired audiences worldwide, including listeners from over thirty-three countries on the *Good Grow Great podcast*. Her message consistently encourages introverted personalities to step out of their comfort zones and pursue their passions with courage and conviction.

In her latest book, *Powerhouse State of Mind: Confidence Keys to Elevate, Expand, and Embody Executive Presence*, Kristie shares her extensive wisdom and mindset mastery approach to leadership with readers ready to transform their lives.

Knowing Kristie personally and professionally, I can say without hesitation that she doesn't just teach leadership—she lives it. In doing so, she paves the way for others to follow, as her life's journey exemplifies the principles she shares in this powerful book.

Kristie's book, Powerhouse State of Mind: Confidence Keys to Elevate, Expand and Enhance Executive Presence, goes beyond surface-level discussions of leadership. It delves deep into the mindset shifts necessary to elevate, expand, and enhance one's presence. The book is not just theoretical; it is practical and based on Kristie's lived experiences— overcoming adversity, rebuilding after setbacks, and continuously reimagining what is possible.

The heart of this book is an invitation to elevate your thinking, expand your influence, and enhance your leadership capacity. The blueprint demands courage, resilience, and a willingness to embrace discomfort. Each chapter is a masterclass in the kind of leadership that refuses to conform to mediocrity, daring you to ascend beyond the limiting beliefs of imposter syndrome and the mental pitfalls that threaten your forward momentum.

Having walked alongside Kristie for over two decades, I can attest to the integrity and passion that permeates the pages of Powerhouse State of Mind. As you turn the pages of this remarkable work, I encourage you to take the lessons, reflect on your journey, and, most importantly, respond with ACTION. Kristie has given us the keys to unlock a new level of executive presence and personal power. Now, the only question left is:

Will you unlock it?

Dawnette Y. Banks, Ph.D.
Founder and CEO
Dreamcast Educational Consulting
www.dreamcastedu.com

Dedication

To the wind beneath my wings, Lamont O. Ward, my loving husband. Thank you for inspiring me to be a better woman, wife, and world changer.

ODE AU NOIR,
pitch black love.
Light up the tiniest stars!
And shield my soul from callous hearts.

ODE AU NOIR,
pitch black love.
Rock my fears to sleep and
awaken my desire for ecstasy.
Drink my secrets;
they are yours to keep.

ODE AU NOIR,
pitch black love.
I have read our story from finish to start.
Catch my panting breath as it seeps through my eyes,
I would freely give it away a billion and one times,
if it were the key to where passion resides.

ODE AU NOIR,
pitch black love.
Resuscitate the age-old belief that chivalry still exists.
As I place my hands in the palm of unyielding strength,
your kiss is as chocolate-coated as it gets.

ODE AU NOIR,
let's light up the brightest night near and far,
with the sacred beauty of our pitch-black love.

The Author's Heart

Your determination, a force more potent than desperation, is the key to your success! At least ten closed doors will proceed every door that opens, but your persevering spirit will guide you through the right one.

If you are serious about rising above the tumultuous tides of life, remember that courage is a faithful ally. Surround yourself with optimistic, not pessimistic, mindsets, and you will find the strength to conquer any challenge.

One of the most impactful gifts I have ever received was a black-and-white mead composition journal from my sixth-grade English teacher. This journal became my lifeline, providing a safe space to navigate the depths of my emotions. Through journaling, I discovered the confidence to overcome my fear of speaking. I began developing a militant mindset to break free from anything that did not align with the version of myself I aspired to be.

As a thought leader in creativity, my writing now serves a higher purpose than self-healing. I have dedicated my insights to empowering others on their journey with tools to ascend above the unpredictable storms of adversity. I am grateful for God's grace, which allows me to lead in a unique way that kindles inner transformation.

I am the truth that remains untethered in the most vehement weather.

I am an endless sea of love to all who climb through the windows of my soul.

I am an unshakable strength that rests at the mountain's base when life seeks to push me off the edge of discouragement. I am the pen who holds the power to change the course of the world.

Dr. Martin Luther King Jr. stated, "*An individual has not started living until he can rise above the narrow confines of his individualistic concerns to the broader concerns of humanity.*"

For the past three decades, I have empowered leaders from all backgrounds with keys to elevate their beliefs to live authentically and audaciously.

This work is a gift to every client who welcomed me into the sacred parts of their heart. I see you. It is for the one who felt trapped inside a job they no longer found joy in.

It is for the person who said, "I don't want to be in the shadows anymore." The soul crying, "I'm tired of being a nobody; I want to be bold." The people pleaser who wants to stop worrying if outsiders will accept them fully. The leader who is internally wrestling with imposter syndrome, believing they are unqualified for the role hired to perform. The mother who has dedicated her last ten years to raising children and wants to feel a sense of accomplishment but is too afraid to make a move. The ambitious entrepreneur who loves to start an idea but stops the second they hit a roadblock. The secret speaker who craves to use their voice but continues hitting the mute button due to a lack of confidence. The dreamer whose spirit is filled with regrets, thinking life has passed them by, but ready to take their power back. The courageous person who dared to take a risk but failed multiple times now sits chained inside a prison of disappointment. If you desire to be one of the sky's most elite, this is the ultimate moment to trust your vision, and it all starts with unlocking a powerhouse mindset.

In our journey together, I *dare you to travel as far away from being invisible as you are willing to allow audacity to lead. There is no place as vibrant as the imagination; it is beyond paradise, and reaching your full potential is more than a feeling; it is the ultimate game-changing feat. Imagine a world where oceans rise to your eminence! The key to freedom is floating inside your mind. This is not just an invitation to quantum leap forward; it is a dare. I dare you to leap over the barriers of disbelief and shut down the internal doubts. I dare you to start a change reaction. I dare you to stand out in a crowd. I dare you to build new momentum. I dare you to create a village for your dreams to thrive in. I dare you to find your bountiful bliss. I dare you to let love in where there was once rejection. I dare you to celebrate every waking moment. I dare you to rock to the music of your own anthem. I dare you to go ahead and smile aloud. I dare you to build from the ground up with nothing but hope. I dare you to believe beyond what is possible. I dare you to scale new heights. I dare you to make your mark and blaze a trail filled with endless power to prevail.*

May each sentence inspire you to seize your moment as you are reminded that every box has an opening, and you can think your way out. Powerhouse presence is cultivated by design and it's all in your mind.

Whichever pathway you choose, go with unstoppable confidence—facing forward today, tomorrow, and always.

Why whisper when you were born to roar, and why settle when you can be unforgettable?

The Artisan of Mindset Mastery,

Kristie

Table of Contents

Acknowledgments — i

Foreword — iii

Dedication — v

The Author's Heart — vi

Introduction — 01

1: The Power Twins of Winning — 03

2: Cultivating Kaleidoscopic Creative Thinking — 17

3: Boldly Ascending Above Imposter Syndrome — 27

4: Courageously Answering the Call to Leadership — 43

5: The Drumbeat of Your Own Destiny — 51

6: Wellness Recovery for Workaholics — 69

7: Shifting Anxious Patterns to Action Producing Behavior — 86

8: H.E.E.L. Yes to Success — 102

9: Embracing Vulnerability While Leading Audaciously — 115

10: Powerhouse Mindset Mastery Keys to Succeed — 126

Introduction

The path of a powerhouse leader is paved with a distinctive set of challenges that are tailor-made to navigate with immense ingenuity. Leadership development resembles the process of diamond formation, where intense pressure collides with exorbitant heat temperatures exceeding two thousand degrees Fahrenheit. From the depths of darkness, the emergence of a fortified gem emerges into the light.

The audacity to blaze new trails, disrupt industries, and advance opportunities for those hidden in the shadows of obscurity must be commandeered with unwavering steadfastness.

Audacious leadership is marked by a willingness to take bold risks in the face of trepidation, unpredictability, and adverse conditions. The commitment to lead courageously is strengthened by the ability to rise above the tides of transition and the discipline to act on one's beliefs despite internal doubts, disappointments, and unwarranted delays. The rewards of bravery received, and the efficacy of audacity revealed after building bridges over the barriers of resistance far exceed the comfort of swimming in a sea of safety.

In the words of Zig Ziglar, "*Difficult roads lead to beautiful destinations.*" What impactful change will you create by leading audaciously on the road of radical resilience?

One of the most disempowering beliefs is thinking you are void of the power to pivot or lack the choice to change. In this new decade of decadence, I have chosen to fling my arms wide open to embrace the wildest highs and deeply listen to the listless lows.

The thrill of embracing change in this dynamic era invigorates and promises exciting opportunities ahead.

Now is the perfect time to begin shedding old beliefs and embedding new ones deep into your psyche. I love Rolls Royce's brand philosophy: *"Take the best that exists and improve it."* We are standing on the threshold of inexhaustible possibilities, and the future is bursting with untold wonders. This transformative journey's potential for personal growth is inspiring and should motivate you to leap into new stratospheres of success.

There is no time for shrinking when you are laser-focused on seizing the moment! Make a conscious choice to be a flambeau (a flaming torch of fire) in the heat of the fight, the valley of famine, the furnace of frustration, and the face of fear.

Repeating bodacious beliefs to yourself and remaining committed to change is the perfect catalyst for a jaw-dropping plot twist

I

The Power Twins of Winning

> "A genius! For 37 years I have practiced fourteen hours a day, and now they call me a genius!
> ~**Pablo de Sarasate**"

The Genesis of powerhouse presence emanates from potent paradigms, prevailing perseverance, a peculiar personality, and detailed practice for proficiency.

To increase the chances of winning in life, it is imperative that you travel with tenacity and audacity.

As a first-generation full-time entrepreneur, I have learned that increasing tenacity is crucial. It is the key to preventing your confidence from crumbling in difficulty. Every day, I strive to elevate my mental state from good to great. Despite what online ads may suggest, there is no such thing as an overnight success.

I currently have twenty-eight vision boards posted on my home office wall, a testament to the importance of a strong mind in overcoming insurmountable obstacles. Tenacity is about holding on, clinging, and not giving up on a determined course of action.

When I was younger, I battled low self-esteem and depression, which led to substance abuse to numb the pain. It was only a temporary solution. As I was approaching the end of my college experience, a few girlfriends and I were at the airport planning to spend the weekend in Miami. There were issues with our tickets and while I waited, I drifted over in a corner to speak with a man shining shoes. In an instant, hearing two questions from him changed the course of my destiny. He asked, "*Are you happy and are you using your gifts?*" I could not answer yes to either question. That is why I never underestimate the power of one conversation.

That was the start of a new beginning in winning. From that day forward, I consciously chose to be a positive role model, empowering others. I began to work on my attitude daily, understanding that every negative experience is an opportunity for elevation, not condemnation or incapacitation. It's all about the intentional steps we take towards success.

Willing to Risk it All

Throughout my young adult years, I competed in beauty pageants. One year, I drove to Charlotte, North Carolina, after being accepted to audition for a fashion show.

It was a twelve-hour solo road trip.

After around ten hours of driving, I was physically and mentally exhausted. I began to weep at the rest area when I crossed the South Carolina state line. I had two more hours to reach my destination. I wrote a song that carried me for the rest of the journey. When I finally arrived at the audition, a lengthy line of women dreaming of being selected filled the hallway. It is considered a cattle call-in modeling, and standing out is the only option.

My menstrual cycle was on during this event. I kept stepping out of the line to run back and forth to the restroom. A main symptom of fibroid tumors is that you have an extremely heavy blood flow that will spill over onto your clothes. I was trying to avoid another embarrassing public accident that was becoming common. Yet, I refused to be a prisoner of my health issue. I would dread every month because I knew an uncontrollable and drastic situation could happen.

As I waited to be called, I spoke with a young lady who had auditioned for Next Top Model several times. She said, "*There is a large group of women who go in at one time, and they call a few numbers, and everyone else is asked to exit the room. That's how New York Fashion Week was.*" I went in before a panel of four judges walked toward them, turned around, and walked back. All I heard after that was, "*Thank you.*"

When I returned to my car in the parking lot, I shed a few tears and then had to shake it off. I told myself, "*I am wonderful, just not the wonderful they wanted. I was a bit peeved, driving twelve hours only to be rejected in seconds.*

If you knew you wanted a size six and under, why would you waste my time?"

It was the first time, and eventually, I would learn that adversity was my master teacher. Show business is cutthroat. I could not afford to take it personally; I continued to show up powerfully. It would become the foundation of accepting myself, as I affirmed that size eight is great! I am a size sassy, and my effervescent essence is more than a number!

The Power To Prevail

Having a tenacious spirit has been one of my greatest assets. It allowed me to go to Bangkok, Thailand, immediately after I lost everything in my second business launch. It allowed me to endure five years of sickness being anemic with fibroid tumors; it allowed me to overcome financial hardship; it allowed me to create my newest company after being terminated without notice; it allowed me to re-invent myself after losing my speaking agent of four years, it allowed me to bounce back from burnout as a mental wellness coach; and it keeps me strong during every changing season of life. It's a testament to the power of resilience and determination.

The world is a jungle; you either fight and elevate or hide and dissipate.

Many admire the aura of affluence but often avoid the agony of affliction that comes along with it.

The flamingo is a captivating example of adaptability in unfavorable environments.

The word flamingo in Spanish means "FLAME." In Latin, it translates to "FIRE."

I am fascinated with the flamingo because it possesses attributes that are paramount for a powerhouse mindset. The flamingos' legs are longer than their upper body, and they are often seen standing on one leg to conserve heat. Even how it stands demonstrates living with purpose. When I was in high school, my body was pretzel-thin, and my peers would often skinny-shame me. I can still hear them calling me carrot legs. The flamingo's poise under pressure is a riveting exhibition of fearless fabulosity and beautifully balanced living.

You are what you eat, literally and figuratively.

A consistent pattern of winning is a mirror reflection of your daily meditation. The flamingo gets its radiant pink hues from eating shrimp containing carotenoids—the same ingredient that turns carrots orange.

Build a future with intention.

The flamingo has the mindset of an architect and builds its nest out of mud that looks like a miniature mud volcano. This beautiful bird can be found in swamps or mudflats, and even with its captivating beauty, it is not afraid of getting its webbed feet dirty. That is the type of leader people will follow to the ends of the earth.

Are you willing to lead by example? My mentor coach told me, "*You must be your first client.*" In essence, become the embodiment of what you teach.

Willing to do things differently.

The flamingo eats with its head turned upside down. This is why being surrounded by a flock of flamingos, aka flamboyance, is necessary to remain protected from predators while their head is underwater during a time of vulnerability.

My first spiritual mentor would say, "*One is too small a number to do anything great.*"

Can stand tall and soar high.

The flamingo can fly forty miles per hour and up to twenty thousand feet in the air. They start running and lift off, facing the wind. We do not have to run from the winds of adversity, but we can race towards the challenge and use it to catapult us into stratospheric success.

Most birds tuck their legs in during flight, but not the flamingo. It boldly stretches them all the way out to enhance the aerodynamics of flight. Every inch of you will be stretched outside your comfort zone when you are on a quest to be your best.

Find strength in the power of unity.

Flamingos travel in large groups in the V-shaped formation to conserve energy and maintain flight efficiency over long distances. An African proverb reads, "*If you want to go fast, go alone. If you want to go far, go together.*"

Become a successful strategist to ensure progress.

The flamingo often chooses clear skies for better visibility and favorable tailwinds. Nighttime migration helps them avoid predators in the wild. They can precisely navigate broad distances, and their strong flight skills help them survive.

Use their voice to connect with others.

They can recognize each other by the unique vocal print they release, which is vital for reuniting thousands of other flamingos in different colonies. It only takes one voice to start a global movement reverberating from coast to coast.

Destined to Lead by Design.

These iconic creatures are born with grey feathers and know what it feels like not to be aesthetically appealing. Like the ugly duckling, the flamingo transforms into a magnificent pink flame of art. Each feather is meticulously arranged to prevent water from penetrating and allowing it to remain buoyant. You may have been underestimated, but a day is coming when you will be elevated onto the center stage of your story from struggle to stardom.

_____

_____

_____

_____

_____

_____

_____

_____

_____

IN THIS MOMENT

> "There will be circumstances that arise to challenge your commitment to be consistent. These will all appear in the disguise masked as excuses. What are your most frequently used excuses?"

5 Keys to Inner Transformation:

How do you remain steadfast, unmovable, and always abounding toward the work of your hands? It begins with a disciplined mind to plow through every invisible barrier until advancement is imminent!

To ascend from within, start with:

Contemplation: Think about what you are thinking about.

Preparation: Gather everything you need to meet the next opportunity positioned to lead valiantly.

Implementation: Execute ideas that have become clear with the spirit of excellence and step over the snares of perfectionism.

Elevation: Your attitude will unlock new altitudes, and as you transcend in unchartered territory, keep reaching far and wide; the skies belong to you.

Celebration: Rejoice in your progress! You have earned it!

In the words of May McCarthy, "*Success is not a secret; it's a system, and it's a system that everybody can learn to do!*"

Your best days are only a few bold action steps away! Counterfeits are attracted to your external appearance, while the committed are aligned to your essence. Wisdom is understanding the difference.

If you were to take inventory of your entire life, what message would it speak? Are you aware of the incredible power you possess? The intellectual prowess embedded in your cerebral cortex appears simple to you but intriguingly complex to others!

> *If you are going to doubt something, doubt your limits.*
> **~Don Ward**

After the bone-crushing dusk comes the delightful dawning of a brand-new day! This is your moment to rise above adversity and reign again victoriously! How long will you make people wait to experience what only you can deliver? Have you positioned yourself internally for waves of opportunities that will materialize when the triumphant tides finally begin to turn in your favor?

_____

_____

_____

_____

IN THIS MOMENT

> Trust your vision. It holds the key to unimaginable power.
>
> "Let go of certainty. The opposite is not uncertainty. It is openness, curiosity, and a willingness to embrace paradox rather than choose sides. The ultimate challenge is to accept ourselves exactly as we are but never stop trying to learn and grow."
> ~Tony Schwartz

You are worth more than that for which you have settled. Even on your weakest days, you stand stronger.

In this sacred moment, choose to let go...

Let go of the scraps of struggle in exchange for the salaciousness of successful living.

Let go of the constraints of fear in exchange for the freedom of flight.

Let go of the paralysis of pain in exchange for the beauty of brighter days.

Let go of the asphyxiation of anxiety in exchange for the exhilaration of effervescent energy.

Let go of the denial of dreams in exchange for the magnificence of manifesting limitless possibilities.

Let go of what was for what could be...

The crossroads of change will challenge your:

- Contribution
- Connections
- Convictions
- Cash Flow
- Career choices
- Creative Expression

Daily decisions are designing your divine destiny one moment at a time.

Definition of a crossroad:

A crisis or point at which a critical decision must be made that will have far reaching consequences.

The point where two roads meet.

Robert Frost, "Two roads diverged in the woods, and I took the one less traveled by, and that has made all the difference."

There are often two competing voices in your head: the roar of audacity and the whisper of timidity.

Imagine the finesse to surpass inconceivable pinnacles despite unbeatable odds stacked against your resilience.

Who will you decide to be in the next chapter of your life?

- Invisible or invincible?

- Lazy or diligent?

- Kindhearted or mean-spirited?

- Courageous or cowardice?

- Silent or Outspoken?

- Average or Extraordinary?

- Powerful or powerless?

- Optimistic or Pessimistic?

- Leader or Follower?

"When you find yourself at a crossroads, choose to be a victor, not a victim."
~Jill Morgenthaler

The slothful prefer sleep over study, sacrifice, soul searching, solutions, and steadfastness, which are the cornerstones of audacious leadership.

IN THIS MOMENT

> **Stop allowing insecurities to hold you hostage behind the prison bars of obscurity.**

Winning is the byproduct of an intentional mindset. It is a lifestyle. If you have become stuck in a perpetual losing state, let's shift that.

Right here and now start to think like a winner. Sleep like a winner. Eat like a winner. Train like a winner. Drink like a winner. Walk like a winner. Talk like a winner. Expect like a winner. Make moves like a winner. Dream like a winner. Prepare like a winner. Build like a winner. Envision like a winner. Execute like a winner. Excel like a winner. Dress like a winner. Soar like a winner. LIVE like a winner. Wake up and WIN like a winner!

Powerhouse Transformation Affirmation:

"I learned courage is not the absence of fear, but the triumph over it. The brave man is not he who does not feel fear, but he who conquers that fear."
~Nelson Mandela

Powerhouse Mindset in Motion:

One baby step I can take to start moving in a new direction today is:

_____

One brave step I am willing to do that feels slightly uncomfortable in my shoes is:

_____

One bodacious step to break through old beliefs and change my life completely is:

_____

Passion for Progress:

Food Choices to Celebrate and Continue:

_____

Food Choices to Correct and Change:

_____

Internal Beliefs to Block Out:

_____

Internal Beliefs to Build Up:

_____

II

Cultivating Kaleidoscopic Creative Thinking

> " The people who are crazy enough to think they can change the world are the ones who do.
> ~**Steve Jobs** "

When was the last time you allowed your imagination to run wild and your spirit to roam free in the middle of adulting? Breathe deeply into this query and allow it to reveal hidden riches waiting for an opportunity to escape the daily monotony.

As an only child, I have always found solace in my vivid imagination. It has been my refuge, a place where hopelessness and despair have no power. I am a woman who has never shied away from dreaming in bold, vibrant colors, always stacking the odds in my favor.

> "We are a kaleidoscope of complicated intricacies. A million different facets of light and darkness."
> ~K.M. Keeton

I will always remember injuring both knees in one of my aerobic classes. This disruptive and awakening experience heightened my appreciation for an often overlooked body part. As an introvert, I am fascinated by the galaxies of goodness cradled in the stillness of solitude. This was a divine invitation to slow down and detox from the inside out.

After twenty-two days of healing with an ice pack and heating pad, I could walk five thousand steps in my city with minimal pain. I often tell clients, "A *win is a win! I will take them in small, medium, and galactic sizes.*"

I decided to break away from my favorite trails and explore the city. I left my rambunctious black and white poodle, Queenie, home sitting in the window. Once I parked my car and chose the path, I welcomed curiosity as my guide. Armed with water, a towel, and Pandora, I walked up a hill that led to a tunnel, and immediately, I started singing my heart out. There is nothing as pure to a vocalist's ear as natural acoustics.

Listening to my voice in the tunnel brought me to tears because I re-imagined a childhood dream of singing before thousands.

> "Imagination is everything. It is the preview of life's coming attractions."
> ~Albert Einstein

I captured unique works of exquisite and edgy art on every corner, obscure to those riding comfortably in cars. On the way back, I ventured to the left through the woods. In the middle of the forest, I stumbled on four huge pieces of wood in the shape of a hashtag. I asked myself, "*If a hashtag could summarize your life in three words, what would it read?*" #stillstandingstrong

In the final minutes of my soul-refreshing outing, I danced as if no one was watching on the sidewalk heading towards my car. Spontaneity is at the center of creativity, and to capture the little big things, you have to be willing to release the rigidity embedded in your own rules.

I grew up in a very volatile environment. Fantasizing about a world beyond reality became a lifeline that kept me afloat during dark times. Out of all the toys I was fortunate enough to have, one remains close to my heart: the kaleidoscope. It is cylindrical and has an appearance similar to a telescope.

At the end of the kaleidoscope, you can see changing and colorful geometric patterns of art that are only visible to the person looking inside. As you rotate the cylinder, a new image appears. The power to pivot in a different direction during turbulent times and transform trouble into a triumphant rise demonstrates the creative flair of a kaleidoscopic mind.

The moment you decide to defy the familiar, you become motivated with the audacity to unleash your artistic imagination, especially under immense pressure treading through chaotic conditions. In the words of Shane Koyczan, "*If your heart is broken, make art with the pieces.*"

The kaleidoscope's etymological root words are Kalos, which means beautiful, and Eido, which signifies the ability to discover. The scope is defined as the space or opportunity for unhampered motion. The mind is a magnificent kaleidoscope of infinite potential waiting to be actualized.

> "A good half of the art of living is resilience."
> **~Alain de Bottom**

How did I continue to stand strong after battling depression, facing personal failures, health challenges, social anxiety, rejection, addictions, heartache, financial hardship, and countless roadblocks? It all started with a radical resolve to fight for my beliefs and the courage to create something from nothing. I've learned to transform my pain into a palette of perseverance. The true colors of courage are the hues of tenacity draped in awe-inspiring resiliency.

IN THIS MOMENT

> " Go deeper and have a fantastic voyage inside the world of your imagination. "

All the angles of audacity point back to building bodacious beliefs.

Me supporting me.

Me loving me.

Me strengthening me.

Me healing me.

Me comforting me.

Me hearing me.

Me restoring me.

Me guiding me.

Me freeing me.

Me cheering me.

Me embracing me.

Me lifting me.

Me challenging me.

Me understanding me.

Me developing me.

Me energizing me.

Me reinventing me.

Life is art, and art is life. When you are willing to search for it, you can find artisanship everywhere and in everything. An easy-to-grasp definition of art is "*the expression of human creative skill and imagination that is acquired by experience, study, or observation.*" The masterful finished work is a fortified strength etched in the statue of struggle, an undeniable result of relentless effort, and it is euphoric..

_____
_____
_____
_____
_____
_____
_____
_____
_____

IN THIS MOMENT

> "Open your garden of greatness for the world to inhale your fragrant imagination."

One evening, my husband opened my home office door while I was writing and inquired about a Paris art frame on the desk. I told him, "*I think it should go on the wall in the small corner space next to the pink vision board.*" He responded, "*You know you can leave open space on the wall?*" I told him, "*This is the vision room; we leave no stone unturned.*" A kaleidoscopic mindset is brimming with passion bursting at the seams. The visionary dreams of what others cannot perceive.

The acronym I established for A.R.T. is:

A-cknowledge the difficulty and dance through it.

R-each for the impossible and embrace your uniqueness.

T-rack your progress, honor the process, and maximize your power.

If you were to step out of your comfort zone, what action would be easiest to execute every day?

I recall a thought-provoking image coaching session in which a client asked me a soul-piercing question:

"*Why am I this way?*" In response, I told her, "*The answer is going to require courage to gaze deep within and unearth what lies beneath the surface.*"

Could it be ... you have muted your voice because you do not value your message?

Could it be ... you hide in the shadows because you do not value standing in the light?

Could it be ... you refuse to ask for help because you do not value a supportive community?

Could it be ... you choose to play small because you do not value embracing the fullness of your brilliance?

Could it be ... you erect invisible walls of isolation because you do not value the exhilaration of loving others deeply?

Could it be ... you blame the world for a life of challenge because you do not value the investment personal growth demands?

Could it be ... you stare at closed doors because you do not value the opulent opportunities waiting on the other side of them?

Could it be ... you rarely take breaks to rejuvenate because you do not value your physical body that is responsible for transporting you to future destination?

Could it be ... you squander success because you do not value being free from the fear of failure?

Understanding the roadblocks to change may start with asking why, but progressive work is designing a powerhouse paradigm that makes you come alive and thrive.

I dare you to explore your entire life through a clear lens, understanding that internal vision is more potent than external sight. The infinite potential you possess is built on the foundation of imagination. Risk aversion is merely a diversion designed to prevent you from experiencing an immersion of limitlessness. The next step awaits your unflinching courage. Take a sip from the wisdom of Horace Mann, "*Seek not greatness, but seek truth, and you will find both.*"

How many lives could you impact in a greater way if you boldly decided to release every inhibition today?

_____

_____

_____

_____

_____

_____

_____

_____

_____

_____

_____

Powerhouse Transformation Affirmation:

"You have to be able to risk your identity for a bigger future than the present you are living."
~Fernando Flores

Powerhouse Mindset in Motion:

One baby step I can take to start moving in a new direction today is:

_____

One brave step I am willing to do that feels slightly uncomfortable in my shoes is:

_____

One bodacious step to break through old beliefs and change my life completely is:

_____

Passion for Progress:

Food Choices to Celebrate and Continue:

_____

Food Choices to Correct and Change:

_____

Internal Beliefs to Block Out:

_____

Internal Beliefs to Build Up:

_____

III

Boldly Ascending Above Imposter Syndrome

> "The butterfly is beautiful because the caterpillar is brave."
> ~**Unknown**

Have you ever felt anxious thoughts in your head were spinning out of control? Do you constantly worry about the future or someone else's beliefs about you or your performance? The whispering voice of self-doubt can start as a small snowball rolling down a mountain and become larger by the minute until it disrupts your entire day.

When we think about evolving into our most audacious selves, building from a rock-solid foundation is vital. If you envision a lavish home in your mind, the first images typically surround aesthetics. It is natural to overlook the invisible in lieu of the tangible.

After brutal winds of inclement weather damage, the outer structure, what remains is the ground it was built on. In our city, we witnessed three tornadoes rip the tops of houses apart in a matter of minutes, and the only thing left was the base structure of the homes.

Can you imagine how different life would be if you approached everything from an elevated mentality? The skin you were chosen to reside in belongs to you and depends on you to care for it, speak well of it, and honor it just as you would a home. We dishonor that which has value when we lack an understanding of its true worth.

It is common to walk around with a false sense of identity if you have adopted disempowering messages from the media, personal mistakes, and misfortunes. I have personally encountered more hardship and heartache than I care to remember. The stripping away of the superficial carved a pathway into the crevices of my being. Standing at the intersection of pain and potential became a launching pad, skyrocketing my spirit into a galaxy of greatness.

_____

_____

_____

_____

_____

_____

IN THIS MOMENT

> "
> Results that are MASSIVE never occurred from being PASSIVE!
> "

It does not matter where you started; what is important is who you decide to become.

- What provoked you to choose your current career path, and can you identify the character qualities it is developing?

- What causes are you enthusiastic about contributing to?

- Have you taken the time to explore the negative emotions that are eroding your inner joy?

- Are you coping with life's problems in a healthy or toxic way?

The willingness to lead with a limp can unlock the doors to exponential potential. Oprah Winfrey profoundly stated, *"When you undervalue what you do, people will undervalue who you are."* Five days a week, I sit with pen and paper in the coaching seat, and the number one confession I hear is, "I have imposter syndrome."

The inability to believe you are worthy of being highly compensated or perceived as good enough is kryptonite to executive presence. Its effects include disempowering thoughts and behaviors such as constantly apologizing, second guessing your decisions, or turning down opportunities due to fear of criticism.

A voluminous number of leaders internally battle imposter syndrome. Which is defined as a collection of feelings of inadequacy despite evident success. According to Wikipedia, "imposter syndrome" is a psychological pattern in which an individual *doubts their skills, talents, or accomplishments and has a persistent internalized fear* of being exposed as a fraud. Oxford Languages stated that "*imposter syndrome*" is the persistent *inability to believe* that one's success is deserved or has been legitimately achieved due to one's efforts or skills. Harvard Business Review explains it as "*a collection of feelings of inadequacy and a sense of intellectual fraudulence that persist despite evident success.*" Very Well Mind says, "*it is an internal experience of believing that you are not as competent as others perceive you to be.*"

At the root of imposter syndrome, you will find countless anxieties ranging from fear of evaluation, fear of not being as capable as others, fear of failure, fear of not having an answer, fear of disappointing others, or fear of making the wrong decision. Albert Einstein, one of history's brightest minds, wrote, "*The exaggerated esteem in which my life work is held makes me ill. I feel compelled to think of myself as an involuntary swindler.*"

You can only be an imposter if you are blatantly living a lie. Nothing is false about who you are as a human being and an audacious leader.

It takes gut-wrenching passion to create something out of nothing! A visionary creating a legacy of bravery treading against the grains of mediocrity every day.

They selflessly pour out their souls like water to enrich others! Most people would crumble under the weight we carry! To my entrepreneurial trailblazers, prepare to broaden your horizons like never before! We pay a high price for freedom, and no one has the right to devalue our genius.

IN THIS MOMENT

> " *The future is worth fighting for. If you desire to conquer the giants of defeat, be willing to wrestle in the mud of mayhem and rise to victory!* "

Self-limiting beliefs will sabotage success faster than you can blink your eyes twice. There are multiple saboteurs of success, yet we are focusing on the leader of the pack, imposter syndrome.

The word sabotage means to destroy something. It originated from French workers who jammed their wooden shoes (leurs sabots) into industrial machinery to stop production. It is a deliberate action aimed at weakening through disruption of normal operations.

Can you see the ultimate objective and outcome of a negative thought? To stop you from achieving, attaining, and accomplishing your goals. The saboteur's objective is to halt and hinder a person, plan, or process from being successful. The subtle intention is to undermine or overthrow an established power. Champions eat external obstacles for breakfast. On the other side of the coin is the courage to confront internal barriers of brilliance created by your own beliefs.

I grew up in a highly volatile environment as a young girl and only child. My dad had an alcohol and drug addiction.

Four decades later, I can still remember the night he punched a hole in the bathroom door, trying to get to my mother. Those were pivotal moments that would shape my internal convictions. Whenever he and my mother fought, I ran to the next-door neighbor's house for safety.

As I matured, it was not long before I was emulating the same toxic behaviors. In all honesty, when I began experiencing my unique pain, I was unaware of how to heal it, speak about it, and be free of it. As a result of my unhealthy coping mechanisms, I became someone I never desired to be again. The angry Black woman with a huge boulder on my shoulder. Mad at the world.

I remember sitting in class during my senior year in college, and the professor quoted Dr. Martin Luther King, Jr., "Nothing pains some people more than having to think." This was my lightbulb moment. In the middle of class, I finally realized that my negative thought patterns were charting a course of misery. Until that point, I was petrified of public speaking which was most of my life. The opportunity to raise my hand and hear my thoughts out loud still brings me to tears. The instructor asked a question, and when I responded, it was wrong as two left feet.

One of my favorite affirmations is, "Use your voice even if it trembles." That day, I discovered there is no perfect way. It is okay to miss the mark.

The Japanese proverb, saru mo ki kara ochiru, translates, "Even monkeys fall from trees." It means everyone makes mistakes, regardless of their skill or capability. It is based on the idea that a monkey may spend its entire life climbing trees but can fall off a limb occasionally.

As I sat in the back of the criminology class, weeping from a newfound joy bubbling up, the prison door opened, and I was breaking out of the cage fear had held me captive inside for years. Adding my voice to the conversation was a defining act that has fueled the transformational work I am honored to facilitate in the minds of others who remain in shackles of trepidation.

IN THIS MOMENT

> " Be not afraid of who you are. "

I celebrate the skill of catching my falling heart before it hits the ground and the tenderness of mending its brokenness when it is ripped into a million tiny parts.

I have had many hurdles to overcome, especially in business. In 2014, I remember turning a layoff notice into Queenfidence Image Consulting. Two days before I received the news, I wrote in my journal, "*I am not happy at work. I want to live out my dreams.*" What a huge reminder of the power our words hold to create a new reality.

In my past experiences of launching a business, the outcome was unsuccessful. I was playing it safe in each new job, and I knew it. I always felt overworked and underpaid. Who was I to start another business with zero traditional education in that area? The most challenging subject in school for me was math. I remember failing the math portion of the college exit exam at least seven times.

They extended leniency and rewarded my tenacity by not requiring a passing score. Persistence pays! I knew it would be imperative to have a bodacious belief to soar above whatever curve balls were heading my way.

I designed twenty-eight vision boards and six vision books to ensure I was a skilled mental sniper ready for any automatic negative thoughts that popped up in my mind.

The National Science Foundation reported that the average person thinks about 12,000 to 60,000 thoughts per day. Eighty percent of those thoughts are negative, and around ninety-five percent are repetitive as a broken record. If you are not deliberate about disrupting your internal beliefs, the dysfunctional cycle will continue. The saying is true: "*What you allow will continue.*"

Recently, as I was leading a fragile soul through her insecurities, the person I was comforting was exhausted from the walls of defense she had erected around her heart and mind. She decided that she wanted to be more vulnerable with her peers. Inspired in the moment, I asked, "*What would you like to add to your wall of protection, a door or a window?*" She said, "*A little window.*" I proceeded to tread lightly, "*If you were to open it and share one truth you are comfortable revealing, what would it be?*"

Deep sigh. "*I'm lonely.*" When we choose truth bathed in transparency, it becomes the antidote that cures imposter syndrome and melts the mask of insecurity away in an instant.

Personal development is the continuous interior and exterior renovation of oneself. We often want to speed through transformation, yet the beauty of our personal evolution becomes more breathtaking with every dare we boldly accept in the face of fear.

"Once, there was a young warrior. Her teacher told her that she had to do battle with fear. She did not want to do that. It seemed too aggressive; it was scary; it seemed unfriendly. But the teacher said she had to do it and gave her the instructions for the battle. The day arrived. The student warrior stood on one side, and fear stood on the other. The warrior was feeling small, and fear was looking big and wrathful. They both had their weapons. The young warrior roused herself, went toward fear, prostrated three times, and asked, "May I have permission to go into battle with you?" Fear said, "Thank you for showing me so much respect that you ask permission." Then the young warrior said, "How can I defeat you?" Fear replied, "My weapons are that I talk fast and get very close to your face. Then you get completely unnerved, and you do whatever I say. I have no power if you don't do what I tell you. You can listen to me, and you can have respect for me. I can even convince you. But I have no power if you don't do what I say." In that way, the student warrior learned how to defeat fear."~ **Pema Chödrön**

For the record, we can include famous people who have secretly struggled with imposter syndrome. John Steinbeck won a Pulitzer Prize for The Grapes of Wrath and a Nobel Prize in literature in 1962, decades after his death. In his journal, he wrote, "*I am not a writer. I have been fooling myself and other people.*"

I highlight the internal thoughts of others who, even though they succeeded astronomically in their respective fields, did not believe they were good enough. They did not have a winning mindset, and they are not alone.

Imposter syndrome is prevalent among individuals from all levels of society.

Who you used to be and who you presently are cannot hold a candle to who you are destined to become. The abundant life is not snuggled in the struggle. It is found in the freedom to flow into a boundless ocean of more.

Are you ready to embrace greatness, infinite possibilities, and your divine destiny? I assure you that it will require bold confrontation of every fear-based limitation. My greatest ambition is not to amass billions; it is to love unconditionally without resistance. The moment you decide to open your heart, walls of trepidation will come tumbling down.

Why does it appear to be a challenge to step outside of a perpetual state of predictability? Our souls innately know beneath the surface that we are hungry to explore the vast universe. At the intersection of yesterday and tomorrow is today, and the question we must ask is, what will I do with these twenty-four hours entrusted to me? This is how you create a life of massive momentum. There is no time to waste, and every moment must be treated as if it is a miracle of life. Every face you greet is a jewel on the journey to eternity.

Sherrilyn Kenyon powerfully stated, "*The fires of adversity forge the strongest steel. It is pounded and struck repeatedly before being plunged into the molten fire. The fire gives it power and flexibility, and the blows give it strength. Those two things make the metal pliable and able to withstand every battle it's called upon to fight.*"

I know what being one of the world's best-kept secrets is like. Innumerable individuals possess vast intelligence yet are paralyzed by petrification. This hidden anxiety is preventing them from stepping onto the center stage of greatness. You were created to exhibit the marvelous works of your divine Creator, but instead, you would rather bury your head beneath the bed. Fear has no power when you recognize that you possess the key to your liberty. You can achieve more than you ever dreamed possible through strong belief and unwavering conviction.

Michael Jordan said his brand was authentic because it was built around who he was on the court, and what he was already doing was easy to magnetize and monetize. Until you realize what you carry inside your spirit is greater than that which appears elephantine on the outside, it will be difficult to vanquish your inhibitions.

Typically, there are only two things we are afraid of: rising and falling. Ask yourself these thought-provoking questions to discover what is holding you back. In the words of Albert Einstein, *"There are only two ways to live your life. One is as though nothing is a miracle. The other is as though everything is a miracle."*

What stories have you rehearsed in your mind as it relates to success and failure?

Do you believe you deserve to live a life of accomplishment, luxury, and prominence?

Have you taken time to solidify the benefits of becoming wealthy and all the lives that would be impacted by your leadership presence?

How will you begin eradicating self-sabotaging beliefs that have existed in your subconscious mind for decades?

You disarm them of their power one thought at a time. If the opinion of others is keeping you stuck in the imposter syndrome thinking trap, I encourage you to memorize one of my favorite quotes by Theodore Roosevelt, "*It is not the critic who counts; not the man who points out how the strong man stumbles, or where the doer of deeds could have done them better. The credit belongs to the man who is actually in the arena, whose face is marred by dust and sweat and blood; who strives valiantly; who errs, who comes short again and again, because there is no effort without error and shortcoming; but who does strive to do the deeds; who knows great enthusiasms, the great devotions; who spends himself in a worthy cause; who at best knows, in the end, the triumph of high achievement, and who at the worst, if he fails, at least fails while daring greatly, so that his place shall never be with those cold and timid souls who neither know victory nor defeat.*"

I have discovered seven confidence keys to rise above the disempowering belief we call imposter syndrome.

- **Awareness**—powerful presence begins with acute self-awareness. In your fragility lies fortified strength and the power to realign on the inside.

- **Acceptance**—embrace the willingness to release what was and welcome all that is to come.

- **Acknowledgment**—vulnerability dismantles the ego and allows you to own your truth by standing in transparency.

- **Authenticity**—you are distinct by design and never have to live in someone else's shadow for fear of shining your light.

- **Audacity**—nothing massive ever occurred by being passive. Dare to play by the rules you write.

- **Appreciation**—harness the power of gratitude and the spaciousness of abundance until the mountains of frustration surrender.

- **Action**— radical results are the by-product of relentless execution in the face of excuses.

The Hyperion, also known as "*The High One*," is a Redwood tree in California and is one of the tallest trees on earth out of three trillion trees. It is estimated to be three hundred and eighty feet tall, equivalent to a thirty-five-story skyscraper. This statuesque tree is full of majesty and might. A unique characteristic is that the tannin content of the wood protects it from diseases, and the thick bark shields it from the hottest fires.

An interesting note in this harmonious song of praise is that the roots can range from two to twelve feet. This can appear shallow compared to the great oak, whose roots span much wider. Nature teaches us how to turn a disadvantage into a prime opportunity to triumph over any weakness. The Redwood tree family leverages the strength of other trees and connects its roots with neighboring Redwood trees to create a force of resistance against the strongest winds. When imposter syndrome whispers in your ear, "*Play it small.*" That is the perfect occasion to let the negative thoughts succumb to your fearless heart.

Powerhouse Transformation Affirmation:

"Sometimes, we need someone else to hold the light for us while we venture into the dark cellars of our subconscious to ferret out our fear."
~Sue Patton Thoele.

Powerhouse Mindset in Motion:

One baby step I can take to start moving in a new direction today is:

_____

One brave step I am willing to do that feels slightly uncomfortable in my shoes is:

_____

One bodacious step to break through old beliefs and change my life completely is:

_____

Passion for Progress:

Food Choices to Celebrate and Continue:

_____

Food Choices to Correct and Change:

_____

Internal Beliefs to Block Out:

_____

Internal Beliefs to Build Up:

_____

IV

Courageously Answering the Call to Leadership

> "Try a thing you have not done three times. Once, to get over the fear of doing it. Twice, to learn how to do it. And a third time, to figure out whether you like it or not."
> ~Virgil Garnett Thomson

The call to leadership and the willingness to answer the call is one of the greatest paths to self-discovery, self-discipline, and self-denial upon which we will embark.

The gems of greatness are individually buried in an oasis of obscurity, to be retrieved when one dwells alone in the cavern of contemplation until deep convictions beneath shallow beliefs are unveiled.

As leaders, we stand courageously at the podium of life with accompanying insecurities, inhibitions, and quirks. We audaciously show up on the front line of change in the face of uncertainty and infuse words of strength into feeble knees.

We facilitate expansive conversations while secretly battling our self-doubts as they beckon us to bow to a life of insignificance. We smile through unspoken personal calamities and climb out of abysmal apprehensions to lead from a higher vantage point of view.

As we collectively experience global disruption, it is more apparent than ever that we need leaders who can ascend beyond carrying a mere title and embody the essence of leading with dignity, integrity, and empathy.

To be impactful in any leadership role, the question is, "*Are you willing to release the insignificant to become a catalyst of a monumental movement?*"

When you say yes to leadership, the necessity of remaining in a state of readiness is unyielding. Infectious energy is one of your greatest internal resources, and it will be hard to transfer that you do not innately possess. It is easy to convey truth when your words are wrapped in it. Trust is easily embraced when your example of honesty is a safety net. Tenacity is seamlessly transplanted from your heart to another is when you relentlessly take action. Endless hours of diligently working behind the scenes cultivate an invincible brilliance similar to a diamond that emerges from a bed of coals.

The highest honor of a leader is selfless service to others. John Wesley captured the epitome of empathy in leadership, "Do all the good you can, in all the ways you can, to all the souls you can, in every place you can, at all the times you can, and with all the zeal you can, as long as ever you can."

In the darkroom of transformation, leaders are suddenly awakened to their unique power to calm anxiety, comfort pain, create solutions, disrupt the status quo, and conquer obstacles. The audacious leader is not waiting for a green light signal to act but understands that what is coming next requires an individual who knows how to confront an influx of unprecedented problems waiting for a resounding resolution.

The definition of resolve is:

- To show firmness of purpose.

- To find a solution.

- To make up one's mind.

- To decide firmly on a course of action.

- To make a definite and serious decision to do.

Former NFL Quarterback Roger Staubach stated, "It takes a lot of unspectacular preparation to produce spectacular results." It is common to second guess your capabilities when forging forward through the flames of frustration. During the fragile seconds between each anxiety-filled breath, do not forget who you are and every life experience that trained you to defy anything! The code of conduct practiced in private will be amplified as you stand in the spotlight of society.

Leading powerfully begins with living purposefully. True visionary leadership requires that you progress from simply noticing to clearly seeing to deeply looking in a specified direction by employing your sense of sight to behold the future while treading through the perplexities of the present.

Your effectiveness with which you lead depends on how well you care for those who bleed at your feet. There was a study conducted by Catalyst in which eight hundred and eighty-nine employees were surveyed about the effect of empathetic leadership that yielded profound insight:

Work-Life: When people felt their leaders were more empathetic, 86 % reported they could navigate the demands of their work and life—successfully juggling their personal, family, and work obligations. This is compared with 60% of those who perceived less empathy.

Engagement: 76% of people who experienced empathy from their leaders reported being engaged, compared with only 32% who experienced less empathy.

Innovation: When people reported their leaders were empathetic, they were more likely to report they could be innovative—61% of employees compared to only 13% of employees with less empathetic leaders.

Retention: 57% of white women and 62% of women of color said they were unlikely to think of leaving their companies when they felt their life circumstances were respected and valued by their companies. However, when they did not feel that level of value or respect for their life circumstances, only 14 % and 30 % of white women and women of color, respectively, said they were unlikely to consider leaving.

Inclusivity: 50% of people with empathetic leaders reported that their workplace was inclusive, compared with only 17% of those with less empathetic leadership.

A study by Qualtrics found that when leaders were perceived as more empathetic, people reported greater levels of mental health.

Impactful leadership presence is displayed through persuasive speech, steadily poised under pressure, prudent decision-making skills, persistence in challenges, and peak performance in various phases of organizational transition.

I often ask my clients, "What is bigger than you fear?" The value that I constantly lean into is empathy for those I have been called to lead. It is what gives me courage to lead when I experience my own life disruptions. If everything is a practice, we can become more courageous with every opportunity presented to us.

As a seasoned public speaker, it is often easier to speak on stage than in group meetings. In those moments, I must practice not allowing my introverted personality to lead my behavior. I set an intention of how I desire to show up and if it is to speak at least once, I aim to accomplish the goal. I want to practice being who I am to the max in any crowd. Even if you choose to be silent in an environment, you are setting an example for others to observe.

Can you perceive a new way of amplifying executive presence if you decided to captivate the room with your authenticity?

If next is now, what do you perceive the world desperately needs from the distinctive way you lead?

_____

_____

_____

_____

_____

IN THIS MOMENT

> " Make a bold decision and do not box yourself in. "

When we say yes to audacious leadership this is when we start owning the sky of our minds. We become air traffic controllers monitoring thoughts and behaviors that support the outdated version of ourselves. As you present your most powerful self to the world what does living in high definition mean daily?

I have observed leaders over the course of several decades and each one provided me with signs of strength to stand in and weeds of weaknesses to pull up.

Signs of strength that I desire to emulate:

- Choose your words carefully when speaking with peers who demonstrate blatant resistance to your leadership.

- Be willing to follow through on what you started even if it demands more than you anticipated.

- Practice the art of curiosity to learn more than you know and gain greater perspectives than what you presently carry internally.

- To foster trust, speak with transparency and humility when communicating with those you lead.

- Focus on the WE not the I. The plural is greater than the singular.

Weeds of weakness, to eradicate:

- Being unwilling to delegate and ask for support to expedite arduous projects.

- Not seeking to understand the unique motivations of those you are called to lead.

- Disempowering your team with an unhealthy set of expectations that lead to emotional and mental burnout.

- Operating in a rigid leadership style that can be perceived as dismissive and invalidating.

- Failing to create a culture of celebrating contributions regularly to foster high team morale.

Are you waiting to answer the call to audacious leadership? If so, what is keeping you in a state of delay? What will empower you to accept the responsibility of contributing in a more meaningful way? Times have changed. The world is changing. How will your audacious leadership change the future for the better? It takes a full two seconds to realize the person who has been called to lead is you. There is not one leader in the world that has it all together. It has been said, *"When your life is on course with its purpose, you are your most powerful."* As you go, you grow. As you grow, the more you know. The more you know, the easier it is to flow.

Powerhouse Transformation Affirmation:

"Knowledge is power. Power is freedom. Freedom is limitless. Being woke is priceless."
~Unknown

Powerhouse Mindset in Motion:

One baby step I can take to start moving in a new direction today is:

_____

One brave step I am willing to do that feels slightly uncomfortable in my shoes is:

_____

One bodacious step to break through old beliefs and change my life completely is:

_____

Passion for Progress:

Food Choices to Celebrate and Continue:

_____

Food Choices to Correct and Change:

_____

Internal Beliefs to Block Out:

_____

Internal Beliefs to Build Up:

V

The Drumbeat of Your Own Destiny

> "You are the conductor of your own attitude! Nobody else can compose your thoughts for you."
> ~**Lee J. Colan**

It may appear dreadful to take the first step because perfectionism and procrastination can stifle the start of something spectacular. Still, the palpable pounding of purpose is impossible to stop, and I am prepared to vehemently defend my passion until the last fading breath escapes my lips.

Deep down in the crevices of my soul, there beats a Congo drum of determination, an echoing endurance that reverberates on the mountain peak of potential from sunup to sundown. All signs point to limitlessness. Do not miss your exit. Now is the time to green light your greatness.

When the valley of the shadow of death drapes itself in garments of darkness, mirroring a black panther in stealth, a fiery fortitude pierces through fear like a cannonball in the air. The moment my feet begin to sink beneath the ground, I hear a familiar sound in the hollow walls of my eardrums emerging from my heart, "*Par rum pum pum pum.*" That is the beat of a dream that refuses to back down.

Sometimes, it feels as if my hopes have ghosted me on the dance floor of my imagination under a chandelier of insecurities. I stand alone, grinning while inconspicuously wiping tearstains from the cliff of my cheekbones. Yet, there is an alternative beyond deciding to run and hide in the meanderings of mediocrity.

I almost tapped out in the twelfth round, but the words of Nora Ephron became smelling salt in the boxing ring of disappointment. Five, four, three, two... and in an instant, my voice shouted, "*Be the heroine of your life and not the victim in this fight.*" A roar of courage silenced the doubt and strengthened my resolve. Limping forward until I could lean against the ropes of resilience, my spirit spoke. "*I know I am not the only one who hears the little drummer boy playing par rum pum pum pum or the caged bird singing for freedom to come and let the dream live on.*"

A comeback is the audacity to confront setbacks that seek to shake, rattle, and buckle the knees of tenacity. As the Congo drum of determination intensifies in the dungeon of dismay, I hold tight to the belief that I can become who I was designed to be. Whether encircled by a crowd or stranded on a secluded lagoon, I will forever dance unapologetically to the drumbeat of my destiny.

If you fully decided to paint a vision on the canvas of your inventive mind, what authentic attributes of your aura would be depicted as you soared to ethereal heights?

I am frequently asked by future speakers, "*How did you start speaking?*" The simplest answer is I started speaking, but it required a willingness to dance to the beat of my own drum. Resembling a butterfly that opens its brave wings each day, follows the wind, and finds a way to flutter in fulfillment. I often return to the affirmation, "*When your why is big enough, you will figure out the how.*" to renew my vigor for the vision. There is rarely a day when I am not purposefully using my words to spark transformation in someone else's life. I have been stringing words together since I was seven years of age. I typed a few short stories on an old typewriter when I was a child, which are now stored in my memorabilia box.

As a lover of language, there are over three decades of greeting cards that my family and friends have given to me. Words are my oxygen and when I feel breathless, each one invites new life into my spirit.

Today, I reflected on why I am enthusiastic about speaking. I found an old flyer where I was conducting Passionately Speaking Seminars for twenty-five dollars, and now, I am paid thousands for a one-hour message. Although I am skilled at articulating prose, my divine connection to God pierces through the hardest hearts, the compassion to feel, and an ear to hear the pain behind the words confessed to me is at the root of what drives my love for speaking.

I archive the emails I receive from women fighting for their dreams, lives, and families.

I often read this message when stamina is slipping through my fingers. "*Dear Kristie, I am trying to unleash the power inside I know I have. I need help. I have this burning desire to speak. The truth is, I am trying to get my life back on track after a terrible 4-year relationship. I am left with an 8-month-old baby and an unborn 6-month-old boy. It is tough, and I'm trying to start somewhere.*" Why do I speak? Not because I CAN, but because I MUST!

IN THIS MOMENT

> "Give yourself breathing space to recalibrate."

What is the one thing you cannot live a day without doing?

I have grown tremendously through this entrepreneurial journey. Each day, I wake to convert every obstacle into an opportunity to impact lives. Every business I have conceptualized started from scratch, with zero loans or angel investors. I am not a slave to my business.

I live an extraordinary life with ample time to do non-business-related activities. There is a more exhilarating way to live when you follow the rhythm of your values. I am not aiming for perfection; my focus is diligence and progression.

My passion for empowering timid and introverted leaders with confidence keys to finding their voice, freeing their voice, and looking fabulous using their voice stems from my journey of overcoming the fear of speaking up for myself. I have discovered through research and coaching that the top reasons many timid leaders do not use their voices are hidden behind these brilliance blocking beliefs:

- They need to be more confident that what they say will have value.

- They will speak once they have overwhelming evidence of support.

- They will only speak if they feel adequately prepared.

- They fear punitive repercussions by asking for what they genuinely want.

- They feel they need to be clever.

- They are nervous and worried about being judged.

- They fear being wrong.

Leaders often express their agitation about not being consistent or easily distracted and ask me, "*What do you do when you lose focus?*" One of my practices is revisiting my mission statement on two pink vision boards. At the start of my leadership development journey, three words placed me on a path of purpose, "**Who am I?**"

- A herald of hope to the hopeless.

- A warrior for the wounded.

- An advocate for the abandoned.

- A seer to the blind and misguided.

- A flaming light for the Kingdom.

Where am I going?

To the four corners of the earth, they proclaim the good news, spreading agape love to the overlooked, the overworked, and the overwhelmed.

"God is in the midst of her; she shall not be moved, she shall not fall, she shall not topple, she shall not be shaken, she shall not be destroyed, she shall not fail: God shall help her rise again, and behold the dawning of a brand-new day!"
~Psalm 46:5

Why am I here?

To make an eternal difference in the lives of purpose and value-driven women.

What is the motivation behind your passion?

I, too, have felt abandoned, alone, and ashamed until God above affirmed my worth and called me by a new name.

Five-fold purpose of my limitless life:

INSPIRE: To fill someone with the urge or ability to do or feel something, especially something creative. Breathe in new life.

IGNITE: Cause to catch fire, especially light up, set on fire, the spark plug ignites the fuel to instigate something.

IMPACT: To have a strong effect on someone or something.

IMPART: Make known, communicate, grant a share of, pass on, transmit, or bestow.

INFLUENCE: The capacity to influence the character, development, or behavior of something or someone.

"She will rise. She will rise with a spine of steel and a roar like thunder."
Nicole Lyons

In the thick clouds of challenge, refuse to allow others' opinions to oppress your optimistic outlook. Strategically convert every obstacle into an operatic opportunity to overcome it and get the job done. Definition of operatic: extravagantly theatrical or overly dramatic.

_____

_____

_____

_____

_____

_____

_____

_____

_____

_____

_____

IN THIS MOMENT

> " You can be the moth or the flame. "

A vision can only grow as far as we allow our imagination to go. On December 6, 1999, I was laid off from the homeless shelter in response to a budget crisis the organization was experiencing. This life-impacting moment solidified my initial call to entrepreneurship.

In the hollow of hardship and the unknown, I realized I could no longer be a spectator in the game of life. It became instantly paramount to begin participating at a higher resolve if I desired to do more than survive merely to stay alive. In creating wealth, we must continually rise above adversity and learn to thrive. In the words of General George S. Patton, *"Nobody ever defended anything successfully without failure; there is only attack, attack, and attack some more."*

This change in thinking happened during one of the most dismal seasons of my life. It is amazing to witness repeatedly, the undeniable truth that all things work together for the good of those who love God and are called according to His purpose. Often, in our pain, we discover the very reason we were created in the first place.

The scope of our contributions to society will directly reflect our personal awakening. Understanding who you are is vital before fully embracing where you are going. You may have a vision, but the more pertinent question is, does the vision have you?

IN THIS MOMENT

> **"** For the love of progress take your chance. **"**

Are you aware of your most distinguishing leadership traits?

As I studied the jaguar, a top-level predator, I found its unique features quite intriguing.

- They have the strongest jaw structure of any feline. It can crack a sea turtle shell.

- Only found in the Americas.

- Their orange spots resemble roses and are called Rosetta's.

- Their name comes from the Native American word Yajuar, which means "He who kills in one leap."

- They catch their prey by the head and chop it down to make the kill, whereas other cats go for the neck when killing.

- Unlike most cats, they are not afraid of water and are exceptionally good swimmers.

- When the jaguar kills its prey, it will not eat until it gets up in a tree. No matter how far the distance. They are willing to walk it out and wait.

Positioned up high gives it the vantage point to avoid anything trying to attack it while it eats.

- What fears need to be confronted and conquered?

- What personal strengths have been underutilized?

- What key tasks are you procrastinating on?

- Where do you need more patience in the process?

One afternoon, during a conversation with my mentor coach, I told her, "*The questions I am sitting here asking myself are, "Who am I when I do not feel like a powerhouse, but I feel more like a tiny house? Who am I when my put-together self-starts falling apart?*" On soul-wrenching days, and I am alone with my inhibitions, I say to myself, "*You're doing it again, blocking discomfort from coming in as a friend. You are melting like wax. It is okay to put down the ax and relax. Permit yourself to be vulnerable. Allow yourself the freedom to have a weak moment. You are still unlearning an old protective mechanism, and your humanity seeks self-compassion.*"

The most evolved version of who you are has permission to be strong and soft. Choose to embrace the duality of your dynamism. This is the generosity I need daily to remain free from the prison of perfectionism.

At the end of the mini pep talk with my coach, her words of wisdom were, "*Allow yourself some grace in this situation. Cut time where you can. Get help where you can, and most importantly, take a break where you can.*" To say my cup was full after receiving lavish validation is an understatement.

I was re-invigorated and ready to lace up and continue leading vigorously. I decided to reimagine an upgraded narrative where I was intentionally guiding rather than grinding.

Later that day, in route to a local craft store, I practiced verbal affirmation and said, "I *had a moment, and I decided how I wanted to respond to it.*" As I walked through the store, I chose to buy a jar of fruit-shaped erasers to remind myself it is okay to make mistakes because there is always space for grace. If life knocks me off beat, I can still dance wildly because happiness is always searching to meet me where I am.

> "*Sometimes things fall apart so that better things can fall together.*"
> **~Unknown**

I can only imagine where I would be without a pen. Around four thirty a.m. one morning, before the alarm clock had a chance to ring in my ear, I opened my eyes and started dancing with the thoughts in my mind.

Cocooning inside my husband's arms, unknowingly, I started shifting my body. He asked me, "*Is everything okay?*" In response, "*It's my thoughts.*" In his usual loving voice, "*Try to calm your thoughts as best as possible.*" There were two options: meditate and put them to sleep or write and set them free. I crawled out of bed to clear my head. This is the story of my life as a thought leader.

Journaling has become a steady lifeline that once saved me from an abyss of pain in the face of suicidal ideations.

The pen and paper have become free medicine, helping me self-regulate. I recently read a powerful affirmation, "*Feel the feeling but do not become the emotion. Witness it. Allow it. Release it.*"

What was the thought that pulled me from under a blanket of love before the sun woke me up? "*Don't allow familiarity to lead to the fatality of future dreams.*"

The first thing I did was reach for my dictionary and search for the meaning of familiarity to see what I had never noticed before. It means relaxed friendliness or the quality of being known from experience. This is where the demise of your growth begins. We often become familiar with our ways, with old emotions, or with an inner circle that becomes futile rather than fertile.

_____

_____

_____

_____

_____

_____

_____

_____

_____

_____

IN THIS MOMENT

> " You can change. You can choose. You can create a life that astounds you. "

The stark contrast between futile and fertile is that, on the one hand, our efforts, or lack thereof, are pointless, ineffective, and without purpose. When we are highly engaged in disrupting our familiar patterns, we position ourselves to encounter a soul awakening, as if we are meeting ourselves for the first time.

How can you free yourself from the familiar and find your fire again? Here are a few daily practices that ignite me from within:

- Every day, I absorb words that provoke me to consider an alternate way of thinking and being.

- Every day, I release the gift of affirmation in the lives of others.

- Every day, I find a quiet place to receive and enjoy beauty by practicing gratitude for the little big things.

- Every day, I stare at one of my twenty-eight vision boards or flip through the six vision books for inspiration and motivation.

The vocation I have chosen is mentally stimulating and emotionally exhilarating.

On the other hand, to ensure I do not return to the familiar land of burnout, I decided to join a writing community where I can explore creativity in a group setting. We are given an image to stir up creative ideas and two writing prompts. In this space, I can have fun and play, which is one of my highest internal values.

In one of the narrative writing classes, we were shown a picture of a train and asked, "Where are you going on this ultra-fast train?" The second question was, "Why was this a last-minute decision?"

I allowed my imagination to escape and began to create, "Today was the day. I decided to delay no longer the dream that set my heart ablaze. I let go of everything restraining me from pursuing my destiny. A friend picked me up in the pouring rain, and I told her, "The fastest way to face fear is to board the freedom train." When I stepped through the doors, my jaws dropped to the floor as I noticed all the empty seats. It suddenly occurred to me that any form of transportation I chose to outrun, trepidation would not be fast enough.

There was a single choice left on the table, and what appeared to be a last-minute decision had taken a lifetime to make. Facing fear head-on is one of the most powerful ways to stop the train from crashing into tiny pieces. In the next breath, I started to scream until my dog barking in my ear woke me out of a deep sleep."

Please be reminded that a colossal world is waiting for you on the other side of familiarity if you refuse to let the fire fizzle out and allow your audacity to lead when in doubt.

Seize Success When the Season is Shifting

As a small business owner, the temptation to parrot, "*Recession is near or here.*" may be extremely alluring when you are under enormous pressure to perform at optimal levels. The opportunity to create a solution out of chaos is tremendous during an economic thunderstorm. Big business impact will demand an updated vision and an expansive awareness to muzzle the noise of negativity.

The first step is to ponder plush possibilities. Simple solutions are often discovered in a sea of solitude. As you design space to contemplate, ask the question: where can you minimize the miscellaneous and maximize massive potential?

Secondly, how will you pivot to present a more potent brand position in the marketplace?

Thirdly, as you eliminate the non-essentials, what specialty product will generate the greatest spike in profitability?

Lastly, progress needs to be strategically planned in detail. How will you identify, measure, and analyze specified achievement benchmarks?

Victor Hugo stated, "*To contemplate is to look at the shadows,*" which are merely dark areas. As you lead your company through the trenches of tough times, be prepared to sit in the shadows, speak in the shadows, stand in the shadows, serve in the shadows, seize in the shadows, and shine in the shadows, but refuse to shrink back in the shadows.

The sun will rise again, and you must dance in the dark until you win. Embrace the beauty of now. Expect the next breakthrough. Expand your ability to blossom fully in any condition.

Be aware of discounting the need to nurture your soul until it is restored to wholeness because fatigue breeds inconsistency. Remain committed to reverberating the power to prevail on the drums of determination in every ear, *"Business is booming!"*

How will you seize innovative solutions and shift beyond sustainable acts into spectacular success? A season is not designed to last a lifetime. You possess the power to elevate every day of the year.

Powerhouse Transformation Affirmation:

"Definiteness of purpose is the beginning of all achievement"
~**W. Clement Stone**

Powerhouse Mindset in Motion:

One baby step I can take to start moving in a new direction today is:

_____

One brave step I am willing to do that feels slightly uncomfortable in my shoes is:

_____

One bodacious step to break through old beliefs and change my life completely is:

_____

Passion for Progress:

Food Choices to Celebrate and Continue:

_____

Food Choices to Correct and Change:

_____

Internal Beliefs to Block Out:

_____

Internal Beliefs to Build Up:

_____

VI

Wellness Recovery for Workaholics

> "
> The greatest discovery of all time is that a person can change his future by merely changing his attitude.
> **~Oprah Winfrey**
> "

There will always be a plethora of areas to develop and enhance in our lives. I have been on an inner healing journey for decades. In my experience, I understand that until we are ready and willing to tackle the issue, it will resurface repeatedly. How long will you delay the inevitable need to change? We can accept unpleasant feelings or numb them with unhealthy coping mechanisms.

The poet Rumi wrote centuries ago, "*This being human is a guest house: every morning, a new arrival. A joy, a depression, a meanness, or some momentary awareness comes as an unexpected visitor.*

Welcome and entertain them all. Even if they are a crowd of sorrows who violently sweep your house empty of its furniture, still treat each guest honorably. He may be clearing you out for some new delight."

As a former workaholic who is enormously achievement-oriented and purpose driven, I appreciate the value of high-caliber self-care practices. I often asked the question, "*Is it possible to be successful and healthy?*" If so, I would have to design a wellness plan where I integrated holistic practices into everyday life as I aspired to own the sky.

Working with wellness in mind is an especially important part of how I lead, especially after overcoming countless mental and physical health challenges. I have a wellness recovery action plan if I start noticing signs of depression or burnout.

As leaders in our respective industries, the demands are unceasing. A pause from the cause is paramount to persevering under pressure and operating at peak levels during adverse circumstances. There will come a day when you stand at your crossroads of change and recognize the dire need to do something drastically different.

When you are blazing on the success speedway, it may feel overwhelming to make any adjustments, fearing you will crash into a wall. We can navigate through this congested place together.

A long-standing pattern may require a radical behavior change. Radical is defined as an action affecting the fundamental nature of something, going to the root or foundation, extreme, something that addresses the major essence of something, or revolutionary changes in current practices.

Are you standing on a faulty foundation or a fortified foundation? The depth of your internal foundation is often revealed in moments of adversity and under the painstaking pressures of life.

After you initiate a radical new way of being, you must train your brain to build new beliefs with a hard reset. To reset means to fix in a new or unusual way, reset priorities, start it over again, adjust again after initial failure, and set to a new value or position. This radical reset requires an uncompromising mindset, which is a zealous adherence to a set of beliefs and values. It is hard to conquer that which we are unwilling to confront.

_____
_____
_____
_____
_____
_____
_____
_____
_____
_____
_____

IN THIS MOMENT

> " Discover who you have yet to become and shift from being a wallflower to ascending as a high tower! "

Step One:

Become curious around the question, "What makes sitting alone with my thoughts and emotions feel uncomfortable?

Am I avoiding any unresolved pain that I have experienced in the past?

Do I need to make sure I have a self-imposed timeline in comparison to the lives of others?

What support do I need to face the truth that I have chosen to suppress?

> "When thinking about your life, remember this: no amount of guilt can change the past, and no amount of anxiety can change the future."
> **— Unknown**

Meditate to ELEVATE Break. Let's take a moment to examine the negative effects a glorified hustle lifestyle could lead to which marketers may not reveal in get-rich-quick advertisements.

- Migraine headaches

- Chronic fatigue

- Insomnia

- Restlessness/Anxiety

- Inflammation

- Depression

- Weakened immune system

- Irritability

- Weight gain

The word meditate means to ponder, plan, relax, and contemplate. Re-centering and regenerating depleted energy can take as little as five minutes. As you quiet your mind in an area void of incoming stimuli, focus on positive words that refuel your soul. I am strong in mind, strong in body, and strong in spirit.

I will never ask you, "How's life treating you?" Instead, I am more interested in knowing, "How are you treating life?" You deserve to live well, look well, and lead well.

Step two:

Create a list of benefits that are the result of cultivating a sacred space to contemplate. A certain level of resistance is normal the moment you begin meditating. Understanding why the change is important will ground you during times of uncertainty and dwindling resolve.

- The beauty of having space to contemplate is that it provides freedom to express yourself apart from public opinion.

- The joy of having space to contemplate allows me time to explore beneath the abysmal depths of your soul to hear the whispers buried in the noise.

- The power of having space to contemplate infuses strength into a weary mind until it emerges fortified.

- The richness of having space to contemplate is actualized when empathy flows freely from a heart full of compassion and generosity.

- The delight of having space to contemplate is celebrated when every breath is a step towards a heightened awareness of becoming one's best self.

"Being silent for me does not require being in a quiet place, and it does not mean, not saying words. It means "Receiving what is happening in a balanced, non-combative way." With or without words, my heart hopes that it will be able to relax and acknowledge the truth of my situation with compassion."
~ **Sylvia Boorstein**

Step three:

Consider each of the responsibilities you are currently managing. Are they in alignment with your top five values and highest priorities? If not, eliminate the non-essentials draining your energy and taking you away from what matters most.

"It's a quiet place, so people talk quietly," said Naoko. She made a neat pile of fish bones at the edge of her plate and dabbed at her mouth with a handkerchief. "There's no need to raise your voice here. You do not have to convince anybody of anything, nor attract anyone's attention."
~Haruki Murakami.

A businessperson shared a paradigm-piercing statement I have held onto for years: "*Powerful people ask powerful questions.*" Curiosity does not have to kill the cat when there are tools that can fill the vat. A vat is a large tank, tub, or container to hold liquids. What is one of the most common phrases uttered out of our mouths when we are exhausted? "My tank is running on empty."

Stroll back in time down memory lane with me. "*What is this?*" I could not for the life of me figure out where this excruciating pain was coming from. It was unfamiliar. I tried everything I could think of to make it go away. I questioned internally, was it something I ate? It felt like a knife being thrust in and out of my stomach, repeatedly with no letting up. A hot soak in the bathtub did not ease the pain. There was only one course of action left to take. The emergency room.

After checking in to the hospital, the nurse asked for a urine sample. As I stood alone in the restroom stall, I heard what sounded and looked like a pebble hitting the bottom of the plastic cup. Silently, I began to wonder, is this a kidney stone? I had heard of a family member experiencing kidney stones quite regularly. How did one end up in my body? Upon returning to the nurse's station, I told her about my odd discovery.

The test results confirmed my suspicions, and the physician stated that I was completely dehydrated. It all made sense now. I began to reflect on my schedule and my diet over several months. In the words of my honest husband, "*You are either part of the problem or part of the solution.*"

I was constantly traveling in this feverish season of my young adult life. My business excursions were not city-to-city but state-to-state. My diet consisted primarily of processed foods. I drank tea and soda to keep me awake for each upcoming event. I would not even think about ingesting one sip of water. My body gave me a rude awakening on that day! I can tell you that I've never had another kidney stone. It was a painful lesson to learn.

That was the beginning of my becoming more aware of my self-care. As a servant leader, it is easy to sacrifice our wellbeing in the name of helping others heal. I admonish my wellness clients to consider that the vehicle (body) is as important as the destination. If you drive yourself to the point of exhaustion before ever arriving where does that leave you parked inside of your mind?

Wellness is an acute ability to protect and preserve one's internal harmony from the disruption of external disharmony. It is the deliberate design of an emotional, spiritual, mental, and physical state of wholeness.

As an image enhancement and wellness professional, I will always remember my beauty school instructor cautioning us to take care of ourselves if we plan to have longevity in the business. There were times when I worked in the day spa, pampering women one after the other for hours on end with no reprieve time in between. It was a sure recipe for burnout.

When I worked for corporate America, my stress levels would elevate to the point, I would break out in hives from the internal anxiety that was building up like a hidden volcano bound to erupt. Naturally, I have abnormal levels of energy, which is common for most entrepreneurs. The one thing that allows us to be extraordinary can also be the Achilles heel that brings us to our knees. The search for a blissful balance is endless.

We do not have to wait until we are worn down to recognize we are worthy of nurturing self-care. There does not have to be a special occasion on the calendar to enjoy a personal day retreat. I love to spontaneously jump in my car and visit a place I have never been before and take in the local restaurants to delight in decadent cuisines.

The wild adrenaline rush you get from having a full plate and the never-ending urge to send just one more email at the most insane hour can lead to addiction. We are an eclectic and eccentric group of elite leaders in which numerous individuals rely on. Today is your day of change. I am not saying it will be easy to reverse old thinking patterns and behaviors, but it will be rewarding. Wellness is a testament to a life fully lived that displays a vibrant reflection of who you are from the inside out.

_____

_____

_____

_____

IN THIS MOMENT

> "It does not matter where you started from, what is most important is WHO you DECIDE to become."

From the moment we were born, the first thing that was expected of us was breath. It is the one thing most people take for granted until life hits them in the guts, and they have no choice but to remember that breathing is their birthright.

Take a moment to assess the quality of your breath. Is it shallow? Is it hurried? Is it being held hostage under the pressures of life? Is it anxious? Is it calm? Is it frustrated? Is it centered? Is it deliberate? Is it soothing? Is it melancholy? Is it passionate? Is it fearful? Is it disconnected? Is it heavy? Is it exhausted? Is it fading? Is it lively? Is it disappointed? Is it lonely? Listen closely, it is always speaking.

Breathe: to draw air into and expel it from the lungs.

Birthright: to privilege one has from birth.

- Be real about how you feel.

- Release the negative beliefs and soul-draining energy.

- Express gratitude for the mountainous loads of work that you are free to execute.

- Affirm your divine worth and what you deserve.

- Take the space to give yourself grace and learn from your mistakes.

- Happiness flows and grows from an open heart.

- Embrace every waking moment to pursue endless possibilities.

Detox Challenge:

During the next forty days, commit to detoxing from all negative media, people, places, foods, and things. Move your body daily through physical exercise. Select healthy, nutrient-dense foods and water only or pure vegetable/fruit smoothies. An intense focus will be critical to completing this mission. Write out twenty-five losses that will occur if you do not make extreme changes over the next forty days. Keep a journal of your wins and mindset battles. Internal shifts create external success.

In the morning, we drink a warm cup of water with lemon and a cap full of vinegar before we go to bed.

Record your starting weight and body measurements in your wellness journal and check your blood pressure daily.

Water is your skin's best friend. Stay hydrated by setting an alarm or using a water app to remind you to drink on the hour or every two hours.

Stretch the body daily for at least 1-5 minutes to calming instrumental music. This will help combat internal anxieties and release pinned up tension in your physical body.

Decide and write out what you will specifically be eliminating from your diet. This is a 40-day commitment to cleanse the body, spirit, and mind. It will not be a walk in the park and to increase the probabilities of a positive outcome find a partner to support your efforts.

Power rests in the ability to use moderation in food consumption. The reason to surround yourself with positivity is because you are removing toxic emotions and foods that will leave open space which needs to be replaced by something greater.

During the first three days, you can expect caffeine/sugar withdrawals, which will appear as headaches. This will require extreme willpower to fight through the temptation to surrender to your cravings and revert to your comfort zone. Pull out your list of twenty-five losses, reminding you why you will keep your commitment. Remember, numbers do not define you. What defines you is the discipline to do what will transform you from who you are now to who you seek to become next.

Move your body! Walk, run, jump rope, skate, go to the gym, dance...do something! Boost your mood and groove to the music!

Reflect and release the emotional weight that is stagnating your motivation. Let go of offense, bitterness, self-loathing, unresolved issues, anger, etc. Stop saying I wish and start saying I will.

One of my health strategies to combat sickness is regular extended fasting. When a family member gets a cold, anyone nearby will also be affected and catch it.

Fasting strengthens the immune system to guard against unseen viruses. When my husband was sick with a cold, an invisible shield protected me. Research studies show the primary indications of a weak immune system are:

- Frequent and reoccurring pneumonia or colds.

- Inflammation.

- Digestive problems (bloating, cramping, constipation, gas), Depression, anxiety, headaches, fatigue, repeated infections, and high stress levels.

To build our immune system, we focus on consuming foods that heal us from the inside out. To change our palate, we must change our perspective, and to change our perspective, we must change our practices. It will mandate an unwavering commitment to firm principles to change our internal posture.

We each have a relationship with food, and it is either healthy or unhealthy. I love this list of food motivation taken from The Mindful Diet by Dr. Ruth Wolever:

(Check all that apply to you)

☐ What I expect from food and the reason I eat is:

☐ To celebrate.

☐ To comfort or to be comforted.

☐ To numb my emotions and distract myself from other problems.

- ☐ To honor my culture and traditions.

- ☐ Out of necessity.

- ☐ To avoid illness.

- ☐ To heal.

- ☐ To entertain myself when bored.

- ☐ To socialize.

- ☐ To get energy for day-to-day activities.

- ☐ To age in the healthiest way possible.

- ☐ To help protect against chronic illness.

If you could change only one thing today that would create a greater sense of wellbeing and peace what would it be?

> *"My doctor told me to stop having intimate dinners for four. Unless there are three other people."*
> **~Orson Welles**

List all the current health challenges you are fighting and research a natural solution for each.

Example: Catching colds often, even during the summertime. A natural remedy to combat the common cold is garlic. One study found that daily garlic supplementation reduced the number of colds by 63%, and the duration of cold symptoms decreased by 70%.

Strike while the fire is hot! Unfortunately, most individuals will not use the fresh winds of momentum to thrust their lives forward.

What does the old proverb strike while the iron is hot mean? A pliable metal soon cools and hardens if the blacksmith delays shaping the iron when hot. The chance is lost.

- It means to make the most of an opportunity while it is tangible enough to be seized.

- To act on an opportunity promptly while favorable conditions exist.

- To avoid waiting and procrastinating.

This is the time to pursue your grandest and most gargantuan goal. Disconnect from lukewarm souls who could care less if change ever happens and are unwilling to work for what they deeply desire. They are determined to remain the same while complaining night and day. At the end of the year, they will still dress the same, speak the same, eat the same unhealthy foods, drink the same sugary liquids, sit at the same miserable job, and look for another happy new year celebration to rinse and repeat the same energy deflating habits.

Naturally, you may feel sadness as you detach from comfort foods. Allow yourself room to grieve freely while experiencing the healing of your soul. After you release the negative emotions, play your favorite happy song. Every time you feel weak, and the cravings return, turn your good mood song on as a reminder that you are happier when you are healthier. It takes constant practice to build your internal resilience.

You cannot afford to sit on the sidelines of success. Get out on the field and be willing to risk being hit by the curve balls of disappointment. As you step up to the mount, whatever you do, never take your eyes off the prize.

Let your dreams be bigger than your fears! Release your fear of failure, fear of outside opinions, fear of success, fear of lack, fear of loneliness, fear of embarrassment, fear of pain, and fear of change.

Keep scoring and soaring above the noise of naysayers because you were created to be a giant slayer! This is the hour to re-fuel, re-focus, and re-fortify with all you might.

Powerhouse Transformation Affirmation:

"Wellness seeks more than the absence of illness; it searches for new levels of excellence. Beyond any disease-free neutral point, wellness dedicates its efforts to our total wellbeing - in body, mind, and spirit."
~Greg Anderson

Powerhouse Mindset in Motion:

One baby step I can take to start moving in a new direction today is:

_____

One brave step I am willing to do that feels slightly uncomfortable in my shoes is:

_____

One bodacious step to break through old beliefs and change my life completely is:

_____

Passion for Progress:

Food Choices to Celebrate and Continue:

_____

Food Choices to Correct and Change:

_____

Internal Beliefs to Block Out:

_____

Internal Beliefs to Build Up:

VII

Shifting Anxious Patterns to Action Producing Behavior

> "Come to the edge," he said. "We can't. We're afraid." They responded. "Come to the edge," he said. "We can't, we will fail." They responded. "Come to the edge," he said. And so, they came. And he pushed them. And they flew."
> ~Guillaume Apollinaire

Anxious thought patterns are typically centered around a future event that has not happened. Forecasting the future is necessary for progressive movement. The downside of predicting an outcome is when it leads to constant feelings of uneasiness which is the unhealthy side of foretelling.

It is common to experience varying degrees of anxiety, especially in adversity. During moments of apprehension, start anchoring your convictions by managing your mood, monitoring the words released from your mouth, and searching your mind for insights that make you feel invincible.

To escape the narrow confines of anxiety by acting in the moment, here are five alternative responses:

- **BE DELIBERATE** in your communication and leadership presence.

- **BE DECISIVE** in ambiguity to prevent action avoidance.

- **DELEGATE** to decrease inefficiency in productivity.

- **DELIVER** superior service and stellar products.

- **BE DISCIPLINED** in personal values, priorities, and commitments.

On July 3, 1978, Aviation Week and Space Technology released a report about an aircraft designed to fly at sea level, and they desired to extend its performance capabilities to fly at least 10,000 feet higher. If you find yourself experiencing negative thoughts or anxious feelings, ask, "Where can I begin ascending from within to stretch my perspective or my steady tumultuous emotions?"

Our brain is one big box of familiar stories. Those who rise above the challenges of life have a special ability (as Bruce Lee stated) to absorb what is useful, discard what is not, and add to what is uniquely their own.

The moment you notice a strong emotional reaction to a situation, use this simple three-step process:

- Identify the emotion.

- Explore it with specific questions.

- Change it with an alternative thought or response

IN THIS MOMENT

> " *Genius demands space to express. Growth demands space to expand. Greatness demands space to evolve. Without space, you will suffocate.* "

During moments of distress, invite the mindful awareness practice of acceptance, letting go of what you cannot control. This can be easier said than done in the moment but it is possible to accomplish.

You can practice acceptance of the following:

- Emotions in the moment. All emotions have a beginning, a middle, and an end.

- Your thoughts in the moment. Notice them and become curious to unearth new perspectives. There is no need to fight them.

- Honor the past and present as they are. Struggling against what you cannot immediately change, often makes you more miserable.

- Emancipate people. As much as we want to try, every person has free will to behave as they choose. You are only responsible for your actions, your emotions and how the current challenge is negatively affecting your outlook. Release what you cannot control and permit yourself to move forward without all the answers.

- Explore an innovative approach. Albert Einstein said, "We can't solve problems by using the same thinking we used when we created them."

- Reaffirm who you are, what you value, and what is possible.

- Commit to taking positive action steps towards a new goal.

How can you extend compassion to yourself and others during moments of heightened anxiety or strong emotions?

_____
_____
_____
_____
_____
_____
_____
_____
_____
_____
_____

IN THIS MOMENT

> " *You possess the power to prevail and have more than it takes to excel!* "

Choosing the most progressive and grounding thoughts will improve with frequent practice. In time you will begin to strengthen your ability to live by core values rather than allowing feelings to dictate your behavior.

Having a ready-made game plan will increase your day-to-day impact:

- Establishing a to-do list is the easiest task. A more disciplined leader must consistently execute assignments and measure daily progress. Effective goal setting starts with deliberate intention.

- Secondly, investigate what efforts produce the highest outcomes and which deliver the lowest level of return.

- It is thirdly, instituting a predetermined routine for completing action steps geared towards goal achievement.

Can you recognize dazzling distractions that consume valuable time and undermine your productivity?

Today, we are bombarded with visual stimuli around the clock. The average individual's attention span ranges from 2 to 8 seconds before they leap and reach for another bright, shiny object. To increase your ability to remain focused:

1) Identify the key problem that needs a resolution.

2) Itemize purposeful activities that stimulate progress.

3) Implement it day by day until the goal is achieved.

How long will you convince yourself that what you have settled for is exactly what you've secretly savored?

Someone recently said they have been drafting a book for over thirteen years. What goal are you putting off due to feelings of inadequacy? Can you count the excuses that you have embraced as authentic justifications? If you aspire to be a leading voice for your generation, it takes audacious action.

Consider all that which procrastination and perfectionism are robbing you of:

- Time Freedom
- Greater Joy
- Increased Wealth
- Influence
- Peace of Mind
- Opportunities
- Strategic Partnerships

The list is inexhaustible! It is easy to verbalize all that we find dissatisfying in our lives, yet it requires a purposeful intention to let go of unproductive thoughts and behavioral patterns. Every day is filled with brand-new opportunities to celebrate internal progress. Do not fall into the trap of perfectionism; it will only stunt your growth and diminish your brilliance. Take time throughout the day to listen to your heartbeat. Does it beat fast, slow, or medium tempo? Release what needs to go and embrace what is welcome to flow. Search for calm amid chaos, Peace in the face of pressure, and resolve in the fire of resistance.

In the words of Anatole France, "To accomplish great things, we must not only act but also dream; not only plan but also believe."

We each have a unique opportunity to improve our world and influence bright minds ripe with untapped potential. How will you rise above adversity and uncertainty with victory resting in your hands? It is time to stop seeking the perfect path to destiny, prosperity, and freedom. The broken road you stand upon can be a wonderful launching pad to catapult you into the unknown. This is the finest hour of your life if you dare to seize every ounce of potential hidden from the naked eye.

My business peer posted a quote online that pierced me to the core, *"Don't look for inspiration, inspire!"* Will you dare to play by the rules you write? Can you envision yourself being the director of your own life story? Are you willing to sacrifice comfort in exchange for conquest? If tomorrow never comes, can you lift your head with pride and say, "I made the most of every second of this day? I dared to relentlessly chase my dreams, unapologetically!"

We often talk ourselves out of success and into failure due to the misconception that it appears out of reach.

There are three types of self-sabotaging mindsets that you must shift if you desire to excel beyond your current state of existence:

Under-Thinking: A mindset characterized by low terrain understanding in which you underestimate your ability to achieve what you set out to apprehend.

Over-Thinking: A faulty perception that questions, doubts, and overanalyzes what is attainable despite past failures and societal labels.

Negative Thinking: A pessimistic view that perceives the world through the lens of defeat rather than a telescope of triumph.

The most mesmerizing moments are waiting for you to move! Where is the excitement in wishing for an invitation that gives you permission to shine? I know you have heard this statement replay in your mind over a million times, "I could do that if given the chance." You possess the capability to create your destiny.

When you recognize your innate value, the world will automatically stand at attention. It is beyond time for you to stop seeking approval to walk in the power of your purpose! Grant yourself the green light and go after what you knowingly deserve.

Ralph Waldo Emerson said, "*Do what you are afraid to do, and the death of fear is certain.*" erity.

Soaring boldly into unfathomable heights will require a winning mentality that thrives on adaptability.

How do you shatter the stained-glass windows of perfectionism and courageously embrace a new day of change? It is as simple as this: decide to be and do something different! Take heed to Johann Wolfgang von Goethe's wisdom: *"What is not started today is never finished tomorrow."* It is crucial to understand that ideas without implementation are merely good intentions, which rarely inspire individuals to ascend to the pinnacles of prosperity.

Grant yourself grace and remember, "Progress is perfection." Celebrate every imperfect step you have had the guts to take. The truth is, we never know what we are capable of until we are challenged. In a purpose-defining moment, we either rise to the occasion or remain hidden in the corridors of complacency.

You are a rare gift to this world. It is time to enhance your luminosity and glow your way! Choreographer Martha Graham boldly declared, *"Nobody cares if you cannot dance well. Just get up and dance. Great dancers are not great because of their technique. They are great because of their passion!"* Finally, I challenge you to accomplish the mission you were placed on earth to do!

The greater your self-efficacy (belief), the less likely you are to disbelieve in your ability to achieve. In bone-crushing adversity, you can awaken internal power as you dare to turn anguish into apprehension and apprehension into ascension. In the soul-stirring words of Jennifer King Lindley, *"Let go of the drive to do everything perfectly and let go of the self-recrimination that comes when you do not. It is the quickest way to become content and reach your full potential."*

IN THIS MOMENT

> "Embrace the change and take a huge bite out of new beginnings."

On the days when you find your confidence faltering, remember the little engine that could. "A little railroad engine was employed about a station yard for work as it was built for, pulling a few cars on and off the switches. One morning, it was waiting for the next call when a long train of freight cars asked a large engine in the roundhouse to take it over the hill. "I can't; that is too much of a pull for me," said the great engine built for hard work.

Then the train asked for another engine and another, only to hear excuses and be refused. In desperation, the train asked the little switch engine to draw it up the grade and down on the other side. "I think I can", puffed the little locomotive, and put itself in front of the great heavy train. As it went on, the little engine kept bravely puffing faster and faster, "I think I can, I think I can, I think I can." As it neared the top of the grade, which had so discouraged the larger engines, it went more slowly. However, it kept saying, "I—think—I—can, I—think—I—can." It reached the top by drawing on bravery and then went down the grade, congratulating itself by saying, "I thought I could, I thought I could."

Five ways to shift from a low state to a peak state of being:

1) Gratitude: You can insulate yourself from the harsh winds of life by planting your heart under the tree shade of gratefulness. Oprah stated, *"The more you celebrate, the more you have to celebrate."* Find a jar or box and write on a notecard the simple pleasures you are thankful to experience daily. They can become a source of encouragement in moments of discouragement.

2) Grounding through Meditation: The ability to intentionally think kindly about yourself and others will cultivate a rich inner peace. In his book Being Peace, Thich Nhat Hahn offers a short mindful meditation: *"Breathing in, I calm my body. Breathing out, I smile. Dwelling in the present moment, I know this is a wonderful time in my life."*

3) Gardening: Nature provides a healing therapy that is often overlooked and underappreciated because of the constant bombarding of commercialization and materialism. Can you picture a more vibrant way of being if you bask in the sweet serenity of Mother Nature's beauty?

4) Growth and Development: A deliberate investment in your personal growth will yield a priceless return for future generations. Operating at the highest level of excellence allows you to discover who you are beyond who you have been. The perfect time to sharpen your mind and prepare your portfolio for future opportunities ahead starts now.

5) Generosity: One of the fastest ways to elevate your emotional state is to brighten someone else's day. Refreshing others in a time of soul drought ensures your spirit is rejuvenated. There is an indescribable gratification that comes from intentional acts of kindness.

How much more fulfilling and thrilling could your inner world be if you chose to live generously?

How can you manage strong emotions and remain emotionally balanced in times of crisis?

- Refrain from responding immediately if your emotions are unsound and unstable. Create a quiet space to contemplate and process your thoughts with mindfulness.

- Write your feelings in a journal to sift through your emotions in a safe, private place alone.

- Speak with an unbiased and nonjudgmental confidant who can be a sounding board, provide loving support, and give honest feedback.

- Accept full responsibility for being a contributor to a viable solution rather than one who exacerbates the problem.

- Remove yourself emotionally and create distance from the situation.

What would you say or do differently if you were an outsider looking into your life?

One day, you will be standing face to face with eternity, and the choices you make every moment will impact your eternal destination.

We live as IF tomorrow is promised while squandering priceless opportunities encompassing us.

We live as IF bending the knee to pray is an old-fashioned vinyl record, floppy disk, or DVD.

We live as IF today is the latest video game to be played with and not taken seriously, numbing our souls with technology.

We live as IF the crumbs of poverty are more valuable than an entire cake of prosperity.

We live as IF our actions are insignificant until the next generation repeats the synonymous cycle of negligence.

We live as IF we are insignificant and pawn our robe of royalty in exchange for a cloak of false loyalty.

We live as IF, we were not created for magnificence and choose to bow under the shadows of mediocrity.

We live as IF our voice is void of mountain-moving potency, and we sit in the silence of apathy.

We live as if we were designed to blend in the background rather than express our bodacious brilliance with high-definition and surround sound.

We live as IF being unique, chosen, and set apart is an unwanted blemish or scar to be etched out of our hearts.

How can a microscopic word with only two letters bear the enormous weight of destiny-defining ramifications?

The next time you find yourself tempted to live as if, remember that a Valedictorian of Victorious Living understands that every decision matters because small acts become the catalyst to creating an eternal domino effect.

IN THIS MOMENT

> " Who do you need to become to manifest what you desire to have? "

Erin Hanson invites us to accept an alternative perspective: *"There is freedom waiting for you, on the breezes of the sky, and you ask, "What if I fall? "Oh, but my darling, what if you fly?"*

We have a unique opportunity to elevate to great, not evaporate.

Hillary Clinton stated in 2008, after losing to Barack Obama,

"Although we weren't able to shatter the highest, hardest glass ceiling THIS TIME,

Thanks to you, it has got about 18 million cracks in it.

Wherever an invisible barrier remains, we will use our vision to see a bridge of unity.

Wherever an invisible hurdle remains, we will use our infinite intelligence to unlock limitless possibilities.

Wherever an invisible obstacle remains, we will use our invincible spirit to overcome it until all have won.

Wherever an invisible wall remains, we will use our determination to reach impossible heights, morning, noon, and night.

Wherever there remains a glass ceiling, we will use our hands to shatter every inch of it."

In 2016, she became the first woman officially nominated for president, and in 2024, Kamala Harris is the first woman of color to run for president. The evidence of anything is possible to those who believe rests right in front of our eyes. In the end, bodacious belief is what separates those who leave a mark that is impossible to erase from those who sulk in a disposition of disdain.

_____

_____

_____

_____

_____

_____

_____

Powerhouse Transformation Affirmation:

"If people knew how hard I had to work to gain my mastery, it would not seem so wonderful at all."
~Michelangelo

Powerhouse Mindset in Motion:

One baby step I can take to start moving in a new direction today is:

_____

One brave step I am willing to do that feels slightly uncomfortable in my shoes is:

_____

One bodacious step to break through old beliefs and change my life completely is:

_____

Passion for Progress:

Food Choices to Celebrate and Continue:

_____

Food Choices to Correct and Change:

_____

Internal Beliefs to Block Out:

_____

Internal Beliefs to Build Up:

_____

VIII

H.E.E.L. Yes to Success

> "Success is not an accident; success is a choice."
> ~Stephen Curry

Before I made a bold stand to use my voice beyond the four walls of my home, I hid my natural talents from the world. It was easy to live in the background, observing the world around me. My mother encouraged me to share my gifts, but it did not always end well when I showed up to participate in an event. I have been heckled off the stage before because audiences can be brutal. During one event, I was performing, and the crowd gave me a death stare. There was no single word or signal in their body language to express whether they were enjoying the music or not. My thoughts ran wild before I knew it, and so did my feet. I dropped the microphone and hurried out the door.

In that moment of embarrassment, a lady named Ms. Lotti came to encourage me. She said, "Baby, you have a gift, and don't you ever stop using your voice." It would take years to find the guts to face my fear, but when I did, I sang the same song, and it did not matter what anyone had to say. I was completely free to express myself fully and creatively. We regain our power by saying yes, even when fear is present.

"I am not scared. My passion devours the terror."
~Unknown

The basic definition of success means accomplishing an aim or purpose or achieving a goal. This description needed to be revised for what I was seeking to embody. For success to complement my inner beliefs, goal accomplishment could not diminish my energy, but it would have to replenish my vitality. As I redefined success, it would focus on being in a state of good health while achieving, being free in spirit while attaining, being effective and happy in a variety of circumstances, performing well while carving out and cultivating spaciousness for uninterrupted self-care.

I created an acronym for H.E.E.L yes to success. It stands for a highly energized, empowered lifestyle. My north star alerts me when I have veered off course and become out of alignment with my highest priority.

As a seasoned thought leader, I am more aware of the weight that comes with being great. One of my favorite quotes is, *"Heavy is the head that wears the crown."* As a radical resilience coach and trainer, I curate an empowering experience in a non-judgmental environment that raises broader awareness around a leader's blind spots and disempowering thoughts.

I remember my first certifying coach trainer saying, "The work we were embarking upon was one of the most selfless paths to take.

I did not understand in totality, but now, at this stage of heart-centered leadership, I enter each day with reverential awe for the human soul and humbly hold in my hands the gift of compassion.

_____

_____

_____

_____

_____

_____

_____

_____

_____

_____

_____

_____

IN THIS MOMENT

> "To create a consistent winning streak, you must be willing to modify your conscious and subconscious thoughts."

I remember years ago hearing a man say, "*The most profitable thing you can ever do is be consistent.*" In a coaching conversation, a client asked, "How do I stay motivated when I don't feel it?"

I have been mulling this over, and a few things come to the surface of my perspective.

The first issue is an immobilizing desire to return to your old self. Those former thought patterns are outdated and will be insufficient for next-dimensional leadership roles. Many individuals spend too much time feeding their fumes rather than fanning their flames. A fear of displeasing others drives an unhealthy need to overcommit, which weakens their ability to go the distance.

I understand the internal battle can be exhausting and falling in love with the familiar is easy. One client stated, "I'm terrified of the future." Building a bridge to better takes unrelenting endurance.

I am personally stepping into cutting-edge momentum that will require a greater demand, which in turn calls for heightened enlightenment. As a practice, I start with the end in view. Before a new year begins or a season begins, I design an incomparable identity for who I intend to be before I focus on what I specifically want to do.

Secondly, it is difficult to be consistent when riding the waves of someone else's confidence, commitment, and conviction. Exploring what lives inside of you is a part of the lifelong voyage. What do you believe? How much time and energy are you willing to invest? When will you stop playing small? What faulty attitudes are impeding your progress? Where do you desire to be in 5-10 years? What changes are you prepared to make immediately?

Thirdly, eradicate any trace of victim mentality occupying your headspace rent-free and be the champion of your own life.

During the pandemic, I was supporting an excessive number of clients who were trying to decrease anxiety, depression, and stress.

At one point, for thirty days, I took a cold shower in the morning and evening to decrease my stress levels to remain mentally tough.

Cold therapy is a simple tool that can fuel radical resilience. The vast knowledge that I possess is futile if I do not choose to put it into practice regularly.

As I reminisce across five decades of success in motion, it has been a wild rollercoaster ride of challenges that inspire me to reinvent myself repeatedly and expand a unique tapestry of transformation.

I believe each career choice served a special purpose, building character traits that cannot be erased by even the most vehement storms I may have to face. The signs pointing me towards thought leadership were always there.

_____
_____
_____
_____
_____
_____
_____
_____
_____
_____
_____
_____
_____
_____
_____
_____
_____

IN THIS MOMENT

> "Set a higher standard to live by."

I recall the last time I worked as an esthetician in a medical day spa. While conducting a facial, my beauty client told me after I poured out life advice to her, "*You should be a philosopher!*" Her statement left an imprint on my heart that I have never forgotten. In my early childhood days, I was the antithesis of a model student and spent countless days inside of in-school suspension. I often dodged anything that came close to the words leading and responsibility.

As I explored what the next chapter would be for me after leaving the beauty industry, I suddenly remembered I had a life coaching certification lying dormant, and I started considering revisiting it.

The first phase was to decide who I would be moving forward in my career, and then I began creating vision boards to build a powerhouse mindset packed with bodacious beliefs.

Nelson Mandela said, "*It always seems impossible until it's done.*"

The biggest obstacle I have faced has always been faulty internal beliefs.

In my immaturity, I would have pointed to an external roadblock preventing me from succeeding.

If it were not for the layoffs, financial deficits, health crises, heartaches, and everything in between, I would not be the artisan of mindset mastery that I am today. I walk my talk day by day and moment by moment.

The coaching approach I utilize is spaciousness so that my clients can be uninhibited in their internal processing. I empower them with tailor-made creative tools to E.A.T. defeat so they can say they A.T.E. the limitations.

One way I innovate in coaching is to synthesize all their thoughts into an easy-to-understand acronym to help anchor in on a value during the most strenuous situations outside the coaching conversation.

A common phrase I hear is, "*Kristie, I feel stuck. I feel paralyzed.*"

To manage strong emotions and escape thinking traps, E.A.T. stands for Elasticity, Audacity, and Tenacity. This is the shift that unlocks the mental block.

A.T.E. represents the positive outcome to signify they Ascended, Transformed, and Executed. This is the result that leads to them shining in the spotlight.

These three mindset attributes will help propel them forward when they feel paralyzed by automatic negative thinking.

In my coaching practice, I have discovered that clients respond favorably to simplicity, especially when they are untangling a problem intertwined with complexity.

Albert Einstein housed the belief, "*If you can't explain it simply, you don't understand it well enough.*"

Understanding the art and science of coaching and the unique niche I have been studying for three decades allows me to flow freely with those ready, willing, and able to voyage beyond the realm of impossibility to discover boundlessness.
If leaders desire to create sustainable change, they must be willing to uproot outdated paradigms and liberate the diamond in the rough by polishing it up with daily discipline until it embodies authenticity.

Our media-driven culture focuses heavily on the external image, yet a powerhouse presence is cultivated behind closed doors. It starts with becoming intimately acquainted with your identity, apart from disempowering labels.

The echo of expansiveness expressed on repeat after a client decides to partner with me or a guest in the audience after presenting is, "*I believe I can do anything.*"

I want to instill can-do power into every heart and mind that I am honored to influence with my inimitable brilliance.

Recently, I spoke at a women's healing retreat, and one of the participants gave me a testimonial.

I created an acronym around L.E.A.P. for them, which translates into "*Live Everyday Applying Pressure.*" to your problems.

The email read, "*Your presentation on reflection inspired me to LEAP. This past week, I have been taking the opportunity to consider my roles to determine if they align with my life's call.*"

My focus is legacy leadership which creates generational impact long after my feet exit stage left from this earth.

Every time a client returns to a new conversation celebrating changes in their thinking and behavior patterns, it is a gift that keeps giving.

May I always cherish it as a priceless treasure, especially when mentally exhausted from being a solutionist.

In the marketplace, I am known for my high-octane powerhouse energy, but what the public is often unaware of is for almost three decades, I silently battled in secret with depression and suicidal ideations during the lowest periods of my life.

I was using mental and emotional wellness tools before I knew they had a technical name.

Each client is different, and intuitively, I co-create with them, seeking the most effective ideas in the moment to expand their awareness and enlarge their cognitive agility, also known as psychological flexibility. The rigidity of thought keeps people ruminating over an unpleasant scenario they cannot seem to let go of.

Every coaching conversation is infused with techniques appealing to the five senses to amplify the maximum benefits of our alliance.

The top three image confidence-building tools most frequently used are visualization tools, reflection prompts, and breathwork for those experiencing elevated levels of stress and anxiety.

If I were to shout a single message from the loftiest mountaintop, I would want these words to be reiterated:

Envision the grandest version of yourself, evolving beyond the pain of your past and expanding beyond the territory of familiarity.

Can you see your radiant reflection in the mirror? A confident leader who is no longer playing hide-and-seek with your greatness.

You were destined to demonstrate what is possible even when you face insurmountable obstacles.

Allow your imagination to captivate your spirit and soar into new horizons, following the wind and embracing the luxury of limitlessness.

When you possess a powerhouse state of mind, adversity will succumb to your audacity and tenacity.

Let every step you take move you forward as you scale unprecedented heights.

Dare to dream, do, and dance to the rhythm of your own anthem.

Always remember, you are free to be imperfect.

When I chose to say H.E.E.L. yes to success it was a gift wrapped in love.

I turn to love when someone acts in a dishonorable way towards me.

I invite love to speak for me when my husband and I misunderstand.

I embrace love when I feel the call to leadership demands more than I have left to give.

I trust love to guide the way when my pain blinds me.

I cannot lose with love on my side in this game of life.

I have learned more than anything that unconditional love can set a caged mind free, and beyond the skies is where I was meant to breathe.

Changing your life is a beautiful journey; never miss a chance to celebrate every moment. Wherever your feet lead you, go with all your heart, mind, and body.

_____
_____
_____
_____
_____
_____
_____
_____

Powerhouse Transformation Affirmation:

"A mighty flame follows a tiny spark."
~Dante Alighieri

Powerhouse Mindset in Motion:

One baby step I can take to start moving in a new direction today is:

_____

One brave step I am willing to do that feels slightly uncomfortable in my shoes is:

_____

One bodacious step to break through old beliefs and change my life completely is:

_____

Passion for Progress:

Food Choices to Celebrate and Continue:

_____

Food Choices to Correct and Change:

_____

Internal Beliefs to Block Out:

_____

Internal Beliefs to Build Up:

_____

IX

Embracing Vulnerability While Leading Audaciously

> "To share your weakness is to make yourself vulnerable; to make yourself vulnerable is to show your strength."
> ~Criss Jami

As a powerhouse keynote speaker, people are often shocked when I reveal how petrified I used to be in public speaking. Even after thirty years of communicating on a stage, I contend with high-performing anxiety. On top of the uneasiness around an upcoming performance, if you add traveling into the mix, it exacerbates the anxiety.

I have never received formal training to communicate on stage. Using my voice to sing and speak is a natural gift from God that I continue to develop with daily practice.

A vocal coach once provided feedback on my delivery and communication style. The words she shared are precious jewels that I carry close to my heart to remember where true power lives. After I demonstrated my ability to articulate my thoughts boldly and unapologetically, she paused momentarily and started to share these words, "*You have the powerhouse speaking down, but I would love to see and hear more vulnerability.*" What she was unaware of is that I spent half of my life feeling like a victim, and I trained myself how to reign in the most adverse situations. All of a sudden, I am being asked to go back to a silent hell and reveal the hurt out loud where others can hear. Simply expressing these feelings causes tears to cascade down my cheek to the end of my chin. I often say what comes from the heart goes to the heart, and if I desire to connect deeply, the path leads to vulnerability.

Over the years, this theme kept emerging in subtle ways, and it was evident when I hired a therapist to help me sift through inner turmoil around my vocation as an entrepreneurial leader. In one of our sessions, I was explaining how I have always had to fight for everything. I had to fight to excel in college. I had to fight through heartache. I had to fight multiple health battles. I had to fight in different career positions. I had to fight in my mind to overcome fear. We all have stories that are on repeat perched in the back of our minds until we disrupt them and create a new narrative to thrive in. During that healing conversation, my perspective shifted dramatically. She said, "*What if you put the fighting gloves down?*" At that moment, I recalled the vocal coach who said, "*I would love to see and hear vulnerability.*"

Honestly, her inquiry caught me off guard, and I knew it would require another reinvention and mental upgrade.

I would have to paint a picture that captured fortified femininity, embracing vulnerability while leading audaciously. I could still be a heavyweight fighter and a happy, wild flamingo in this new reality. Therapy with Sherri taught me that there is space for more than one choice.

I started practicing welcoming vulnerability to decrease high-performance anxiety and increase inner peace. She told me, "The pressure to perform perfectly has to be tiring." An insightful way of being for me is recognizing that I do not have to power forward to perform well, and with gentleness, I can still be present for myself when I need to heal.

In the excitement of creating an inspiring movement, I reiterate an important message: "As you build, don't forget to breathe with ease."

For several months, I have been in a season of quiet contemplation, spending my weekends in botanical gardens or by the ocean to capture the softest whisper between the winds of wandering. In the same year as turning fifty, I was preparing to have surgery for a similar health issue that was extremely debilitating twelve years ago.

Recently, during my time of reflection, I revisited this familiar thought, "*If I embrace vulnerability, will it decrease the agony of anxiety?*" I have trained my spirit and mind to be strong, but what still requires an enormous amount of practice is sitting with emotional frailty. I went to the hospital for pre-op appointments, and when they put the identification bracelet on my wrist, tears began to fall down my face. I did not have a single tissue to wipe my face. I pulled my t-shirt up to my eyes until they were dried.

The choice I made is clear. The operation date and the extensive list of to-dos and not-to-dos were overwhelming.

Between the upcoming surgery and preparing to teach my life coach students, I stumbled across a manilla folder with poetic prose tucked inside. I forgot I penned it as an encouragement to myself on April 8, 2023.

It was late in the evening; I found myself curled up inside a blanket of disappointment after missing a passing score on the ICF coaching credential exam by twenty-one points. The first time I took the exam, the testing center computer crashed, and my exam vanished into thin air. This had been a two-year training process, and now I would have to take the test for a third time. In a fleeting moment of frustration, I found a new resolve, and four months later August 24, 2023, I received the reward of countless hours invested by successfully passing the test. I am enrolled in the Master Certified Coach training program, daring to traverse another rigorous path of high-level skill development.

One year later, life continues to teach me that I can make a positive impact from a hard place, a high place, a strong place, a tender place, a lonely place, a loving place, a courageous place, a fearful place, an abundant place, and an insufficient place. I am learning to embrace and celebrate the perseverance of planting one foot in front of the other day by day.

IN THIS MOMENT

> "When my heart and mind speak, I choose to sit and listen. After swimming in a sea of solitude, I step onto the shore of serenity, ready to create my next move."

Fiery Fortitude and Forward Focus

"You can either see yourself as a wave in the ocean, or you can see yourself as the ocean."
~Oprah Winfrey

One ocean contains three hundred and fifty-two quintillion gallons of water. The human spirit is limitless. It is our beliefs that often bulldoze our dreams from under our feet.

As I was driving to Aqua aerobics early one morning, I began to think how different my life is one week after releasing myself from an employment contract providing emotional and mental wellness coaching. The space that once filled me to the overflow was beginning to weigh down my soul. In therapy with Sherri, she would say, "*It is just temporary. You are choosing to stay.*" Suddenly, it was clear. If I chose to stay, then I could also choose to leave. One of my favorite affirmations is, "*Everything is figureoutable.*"

I believe in living by my values, and when I step outside of my core principles, it cannot be ignored for long because the whisper turns into a roar. For three months, I felt disempowered and heavy in heart. Internally, I was living contrary to my message of audacious leadership. The best way to care for others is to first care for yourself.

A simple sign that you are out of alignment with your authentic self is typically revealed in your energy levels. Environmental wellness and its impact on our emotional state are often overlooked. A decision had to be made while searching for the next best course of action to take in my career. My husband told me years ago, "*You have the power to stop your hemorrhaging.*" It was unwise for me to think that I would be able to heal in the same place that was making me sick. Your environment can either amplify your energy by igniting and intensifying it or capsizing it to the point of drowning and draining it.

_____

_____

_____

_____

_____

_____

_____

_____

IN THIS MOMENT

> " I release the need to be there before I get there. The answers will be clear to see and to me. "

Clients frequently struggle with the fear, "What if I don't make the right choice?" I asked them, "What if there were no wrong choices?" In the words of Joseph Campbell, "We must be willing to let go of the life we planned to have, the life that is waiting for us." At the center of indecision is a thought that needs to be acknowledged and addressed, and the audacity to act bravely in the moment.

Everyone has their ways of coping with the challenges of life. A common way to self-soothe is by avoiding what is hard to face head-on. We decide not to decide and that only intensifies the volcanic emotions waiting to erupt at any given time of the day.

The path of purpose is often revealed in between the moments and movements. The word path is defined as a track laid down for walking or made by continual treading, the course or direction in which a person is moving, or a choice or way of living. Garth Nix asked a powerful question for the pioneer of purpose paving their own unique path: "Does the walker choose the path, or does the path choose the walker?"

In my stillness, I started flipping through an old journal and noticed a movie quote that I had forgotten about. It was called The Art of Us, and one of the characters said, "*How you spend your days matters more than how it pays.*" That was another permission slip reminding me it was time to leave, especially since I was becoming increasingly unhappy. I have supported thousands of clients transitioning from one career role into the next and my moment to leap into the unknown had arrived.

As I envisioned a new plan, I remembered a female leader telling me, "*Every organization has a pinch point, and you have to decide when it gets too pinchy for you to stay.*" It was not until I created a new story in my mind that I experienced the opposite of feeling trapped and stepped into the vulnerability of not knowing what the future holds.

Today, I am lighter and happier, figuring it out breath by breath and step by step. Understanding that the unfolding of the vision can be imperfect allows me to skip through the fields of my imagination with childlike joy. In every breath we inhale, there is a gift called receiving, and with every wind of air exhaled, we call it releasing.

"Breathe, darling. This is just a chapter. It's not your whole story."
~S.C. Lourie

_____
_____
_____
_____

IN THIS MOMENT

> " I am re-designing a life that is abounding in abundance. The oceans are calling me, and with brave, open wings, I am soaring completely free. "

Nature is a constant source of inspiration when I feel weary from leadership obligations. Every day, I walk with my dog Queenie around the neighborhood, and on one of our strolls, the wispy part of the dandelion came flying by. I picked it up and started blowing on it like I did as a child. When I returned to my home office, I immediately started researching the qualities of the dandelion. It symbolizes resilience, emotional healing, and hope in several cultures and can be used to treat infections, inflammation, and liver problems. The French word is Dents De Lion, meaning the teeth of a lion.

The dandelion can grow in almost any environment regardless of the soil conditions. Each dandelion can produce up to twenty thousand viable seeds. They can endure hot and cold climates. If a fire scorches the land, one of the first flowers to appear again will be the dandelion. They can regrow repeatedly because their roots run six to twelve feet deep.

When you are experiencing a period of vulnerability, wrap yourself in resiliency and allow your strength to be electrified by adaptability.

The dandelion can transform from a bright yellow flower into a delicate white wispy seed head that has up to three hundred tiny pedals called pappi. These seeds sail in the wind to plant new roots wherever they land next.

Wherever your feet stand today, refuse to allow your dreams to sleep in the darkness of disappointment. Bring them into the daylight of determination.

Let your dreams unlock the potency of your potential in the manifested power to endure the fiery furnace that produces a relentless and unyielding fortitude.

Dance in the fields of your dreams and spin around in the joy of a heart that overflows with the richness of gratitude and an unconquerable hope against all obstacles.

Kiss the face of your dreams as you breathe in the audacity to rise.

Walk together with the faithfulness of God, who is the giver of dreams and never slumbers nor sleeps on your divine destiny.

_____

_____

_____

_____

_____

_____

Powerhouse Transformation Affirmation:

"The world will tell you how to live if you let it. Do not let it! Take up your space. Raise your voice. Sing your song. This is your chance to make or re-make a life that THRILLS YOU!"
~Shauna Niequist

Powerhouse Mindset in Motion:

One baby step I can take to start moving in a new direction today is:
___

One brave step I am willing to do that feels slightly uncomfortable in my shoes is:
___

One bodacious step to break through old beliefs and change my life completely is:
___

Passion for Progress:

Food Choices to Celebrate and Continue:
___

Food Choices to Correct and Change:
___

Internal Beliefs to Block Out:
___

Internal Beliefs to Build Up:
___

X

Powerhouse Mindset Mastery Keys to Succeed

> "You were created to do good work. Work that empowers and inspires, liberates, and transforms, restores, and softens. Yes, work can be hard as it was meant to be. The verb itself calls us into action. It is rejecting passivity and demanding sustained effort. It provokes, agitates, and disturbs. But this work calls for justice- it is good work. It defends the oppressed and frees the captive. It tears down walls and destroys barriers. It changes things. So, when you are feeling weary, hopeless, or spent, remind yourself that the darkness is being flooded by marvelous light. Yes, this is work. And it is good."
> ~Danielle Coke

In my home office, on a three-by-five note card, is a note to self that reads:

Daily Focus: Ignite Hearts, Inspire Minds, and Impact Lives. It is my compass that keeps me centered on purposeful living. As I reflect on thousands of conversations with leaders who desired to communicate more confidently, make space to date, lose weight, heal a heart ache, or think more positively there was one thing I noticed. The clients who obtained the best results by far were the ones who started implementing tools to build new beliefs and behaviors.

When I step on a stage full of electrifying energy, what feeds that energy are my private practices. I have spent days in nature, journaling, listening to instrumental music, group fitness and anything that rebalances me internally. I cannot count the number of times I have said to a client, "The power is in practice." It is human nature to want rapid results. After three plus decades of personal development, I am still working on my tools. In this concluding chapter, as you discover new tools, I challenge you to commit to the power of regular practice for maximum impact.

Powerhouse Manifesto

Powerhouse Physique: How do you desire to appear aesthetically?

Powerhouse Profitability: What services or products will you produce for the marketplace to accelerate financial increase?

Powerhouse Paradigm: What cognitive shifts in mindset do you need to resist or allow to persist?

Powerhouse Partnerships: Who are the high-caliber leaders you seek to collaborate with?

Powerhouse Palate: What new food choices will impact you wholistically and energetically?

Powerhouse Palace: How can you create an environment that attracts greater degrees of luxury in your living abode?

Powerhouse Playtime: What soul-enriching activities will replenish your energy and creativity?

_____

_____

_____

_____

_____

Powerhouse Prompts to Ponder

Stagnancy results from faulty beliefs or fruitless behavior, and decisions are the designers of a dynamic destiny.

- When I am in a powerhouse state of mind, I choose...
- When I am in a powerhouse state of mind, the world around me...
- When I am in a powerhouse state of mind, I expect...
- What do I need to stop denying that...
- The truth is...
- I choose to start believing...
- My life is a....
- My deepest purpose is to be...
- I am willing to let go of...and welcome more of ... into my life.
- When I am in a powerhouse state of mind, I feel...

_____
_____
_____

Powerhouse Inner Reflection

- Where do I need to reinvest time and energy?

- What aspect of myself do I need to reinvent?

- How will I reenergize my body?

- What action do I need to recommit to?

- If next is now, what do you perceive the world desperately needs from the unique way you lead?

- What daily disciplines can I implement to expand consciousness and attract higher quality life experiences?

- What new decisions am I ready, willing, and able to make?

- What daily delights and detours am I willing to appreciate?

- What areas of my life have I been shrinking back instead of stepping forward?

_____

_____

_____

_____

10 Ways to Elevate to Great Every Day: (Self-Check List)

ENVIRONMENT: Does it heighten or diminish internal stress?

EXCHANGES: Humility is learning from anyone and anything. Am I maximizing personal connections and creating engaging dialogue throughout the day?

EXPECTATIONS: Are my beliefs high or low? Where do I need to ascend in my thought processes?

ENERGY: Am I energy proficient or deficient? Who or what is stifling my vitality?

ENDEAVORS: Are my activities strategically aligned with my values, vision, and verity?

EMBRACING the EXITS: Do I harbor any disappointment around what did not transpire or who is absent from my presence?

EATING: Is my nutritional plan filled with foods that fuel my productivity for optimal performance, emotional wellness, and mental nourishment?

ELIMINATION: What unproductive behavior patterns must be eradicated and elevated?

EVERYDAY: Do I intentionally and freely give thanks for everything, or do I feel entitled to a life of ease?

EXERCISE: Am I exercising regularly to increase blood flow, strengthen joints, and boost a feel-good mood?

Power Pause

Breath upon breath, let the heavyweights fall off my chest.

- What is NOW?
- What is NECESSARY?
- What is NON-ESSENTIAL?
- What is NEXT?

_____
_____
_____
_____
_____
_____
_____
_____
_____
_____
_____

Powerhouse State of Mind Affirmations

- I am magnetic to the max.

- Practice makes polished, and polished makes profits.

- I am manifesting suddenly, expectantly, and undeniably.

- I am excited about my future fortune now.

- It is coming by the hundreds, thousands, millions, billions, and trillions.

- I embrace infinite possibilities and unstoppable prosperity.

- I will exude resilience.

- I will exude elevated energy.

- I will exude bodacious belief.

- I will exude compassion.

- I will exude freedom and flow.

- I will exude limitless possibilities.

- I will exude brilliance.

- I will exude extraordinary leadership.

- I will exude greatness.

- I will exude success.
- I will exude passion for purpose.
- I will exude determination towards my goals.
- I will exude magnificence.
- I will exude happiness and joy.
- I will be the magnet and manifest abundance.

Powerhouse Peak Performance Energy Affirmations:

- Exhausted energy attracts poverty, and elevated energy attracts luxury and manifests prosperity.
- I eat in a way that deeply supports my health and reflects my best self.
- I move for energy.
- I speak for energy.
- I color for energy.
- I listen to music for energy.
- I read for energy.
- I connect with high-value leaders for energy.
- I sit in nature for energy.
- I meditate for energy.
- I breathe deep for energy.
- I rest for energy.
- I detox for energy.
- I live for energy.
- I am pure energy.
- I give thanks for what was, for what is, and for what is coming in exponential portions.

Powerhouse Mega Vision Affirmations

- I see high-caliber connections and high-end clients.
- I see elevated experiences beyond my comprehension.
- I see all expense-paid exotic travel destinations.
- I see a new passion for purpose.
- I see divine wisdom, knowledge, and understanding.
- I see uncommon creative abilities flowing through me.
- I see supernatural power and authority.
- I see wealth, abundance, and prosperity.
- I see unprecedented favor over every interaction and opportunity.
- I see nothing missing and nothing broken.
- I see freedom, love, and unspeakable joy!
- I see a cutting-edge prophetic ax abolishing iron barriers of lack.
- I see an unbeatable strength to stand against the fiercest winds of opposition.

Powerhouse Style Affirmations

- When working, I wear green to allow money to flow freely.

- When creating new connections, I wear orange to express my effervescent personality.

- When I am on stage presenting, I wear black for buoyant brilliance.

- When I'm on a date with destiny, I wear red lady luxe, which is too hot to trot.

- When traveling worldwide, I wear blue, for the sky is not the limit.

- When exercising, I wear purple to reign in my divine domain.

- When preparing for bed, I wear a leopard print for what comes next.

- When I am standing at the crossroads of a decision, I wear pink for purpose is my power.

- I wear bold gold when my confidence is low to amplify a magnetic shine that I cannot hide.

Powerhouse Personal Declaration of Rights

- You have the right to speak from your innermost being.
- You have the right to fall deeply in love without reservation or complication.
- You have the right to be whole in every fiber of your mind, body, and soul.
- You have the right to change directions and make a different decision.
- You have the right to dream without measure.
- You have the right to receive high-level support.
- You have the right to dance in wild happiness and ecstatic joy.
- You have the right to have your generosity reciprocated.
- You have the right to decline opportunities incongruent with your core values.
- You have the right to be selective about who you invest valuable time with.
- You have the right to live by design and not by default.
- You have the right to explore your potential to the fullest.

- You have the right to walk boldly in uncommon favor, prosperity, and territories.

- You have the right to build thriving, loving, and healthy relationships.

- You have the right to pave new paths and open new doors.

- You have the right to protect what is sacred from the snares of the fowler.

- You have the right to trust but verify the authenticity of motives disguised as little lies.

- You have the right to be a distinct diamond of determination.

- You have the right to breathe freely and remain unchained from public opinion.

- You have the right to embrace the power to prevail and unleash prayers that shake the gates of hell.

- How will you exercise your divine rights while refusing to remain silent in this clamoring world?

_____

_____

_____

_____

_____

Powerhouse Action Plan

Visualize Your Best Self Exercise:

- Begin with the end in mind and make it happen now. Write out the specific change you expect in the next 24 hours, 7 days, 2 weeks, or 1 month from today.

- Design a vision board, book, or statement about your expected accomplishment.

- Purchase an accountability journal to log daily thoughts and milestones achieved.

- Establish your support system and surround yourself with positive people who believe in you.

- Pre-record audio words of inspiration to yourself to hear daily to reinforce your new lifestyle goals.

- Eliminate all traces of unhealthy food or drinks in your home and replace them with healthy alternatives that reflect your new desires.

- Celebrate each accomplishment, big or small, and reward yourself with a smiley face on a dry-erase calendar placed on your refrigerator to witness personal progress.

_____

_____

Powerhouse Wellness Regime

I will watch my water intake. Continually think of ways to set yourself up for success. Keep a bottle of water on your nightstand to drink upon waking. Place a container near your workstation if you work long hours in front of a desk.

I will move throughout my day. It is easy to become sedentary, especially with an office job. Challenge yourself to take the stairs rather than the elevator. Seek to incorporate at least 15-30 minutes of physical activity daily. You will begin to see a boost in your mood and productivity.

I will eat whole foods. When you first change your diet, it is more effective to add whole foods, and you may inadvertently start decreasing processed foods. Focus on the good as you naturally create a new habit. Remember, minor changes can produce massive results! Where there is determination, there is a door that opens to a delightful destination.

I will spend quality time alone. Typically, our days are consumed with massive to-do lists and non-stop requests. There will always be assignments waiting to be attended to. The key is intentionally seizing moments of solace to reignite your internal fire.

_____
_____
_____
_____

I will create a peaceful dwelling environment. Design your home to be a calm habitation that you can retreat to after battling the cares of the world. Surround your living space with scented candles that warm the soul. Play instrumental music to soothe any feelings of tension and anxiety. In addition, pour a few drops of one of your favorite essential oils on a wet towel and warm it up in the microwave for a couple of minutes. Position the towel around your neck and inhale the aroma until the scent dissipates.

I will invest in friend therapy. There is no better medicine than being in the company of a good friend. They house a wellspring of love that refreshes our barren souls. At least once a week, connect with a friend in a meaningful way that leaves you rejuvenated.

I will take a bubble bath. It is easy to jump in and out of the shower. Women on the move seeking to quickly get back into action find this option to work well for their schedule. The art of soaking reminds us to be still within and gently love ourselves, know ourselves, and treat ourselves like a five star hotel guest in our own home.

_____

_____

_____

_____

_____

_____

_____

Powerhouse Emotional Empowerment

Your emotions are not your enemies. Create space to sit with them and deeply listen to what they want to say.

- What do you hear?
- What do you fear?
- What do you want to cheer?
- What direction will you choose to steer?
- What are you withholding from yourself due to being distracted by the now and near?

What is your superpower?

Every IT girl has a unique I.T. Factor!

Identity: Who am I, why am I here, and what do I want to leave as a legacy to those who follow my lead?

I.M. (A) G.E. I'm a great example of_____.

Tell your story. Maya Angelou said that there is nothing more agonizing than bearing in your soul an untold story.

_____

_____

Grasp every growth opportunity tightly and collect rare wisdom jewels for the journey.

Infuse well-being into daily living and ignite your fire.

A roadmap to better. Visualize what next looks like. You possess the power to design an open door of opportunity by using pure imagination.

Lead to win. Lead to impact. Lead to new horizons.

_____

_____

_____

_____

_____

_____

_____

_____

_____

_____

_____

_____

Powerhouse Transformation Affirmation:

"The day came when the risk to remain tight in a bud was more painful than the risk it took to blossom."
~Anais Nin

Powerhouse Mindset in Motion:

One baby step I can take to start moving in a new direction today is:

_____

One brave step I am willing to do that feels slightly uncomfortable in my shoes is:

_____

One bodacious step to break through old beliefs and change my life completely is:

_____

Passion for Progress:

Food Choices to Celebrate and Continue:

_____

Food Choices to Correct and Change:

_____

Internal Beliefs to Block Out:

_____

Internal Beliefs to Build Up:

Purpose and Progress Check-In

Rock:

What feels as if it is too heavy to lift right now?

Paper:

What would make me feel light as a kite?

Scissors:

What needs alteration or elimination from my daily routine or life completely?

_____
_____
_____
_____
_____
_____
_____
_____

As we close the curtains of our time together, remember it starts with a spark. The next decision is a commitment to keep fanning the flames of your passion every day or as often as you can to prevent stagnancy from creeping in between your steps to destiny.

The journey of personal transformation is one of the most intimate paths of self-discovery upon which you will embark. It is filled with rich rewards and the most arduous challenges.

Now is the time to astonish yourself and demonstrate what you are made of. The world is your stage; I dare you to take the lead and broadcast your brilliance in your sphere of influence.

"These words I speak to you are not incidental additions to your life, homeowner improvements to your standard of living. They are foundational words, words to build a life on. If you work these words into your life, you are like a smart carpenter who built his house on solid rock. Rain poured down, the river flooded, and a tornado hit—but nothing moved that house. It was fixed to the rock." Matthew 7:24-27 The Message

Synopsis

Imagine ...The clarity to act. The courage to lead. The confidence to excel.

We are standing on the threshold of limitless possibilities and the future is bursting with wonders untold.

Powerhouse State of Mind is a dynamic empowerment tool for introverted and emerging leaders. Each chapter is designed to crush hidden fears, build bodacious belief, and ignite an unstoppable flame of fire to pursue deep-seated desires. Answering the courageous call to leadership demands tenacity, and not taking risks is risky! Daring is a masterful art of the brave hearted. Big dreams demand big determination.

It is easy to skate quietly around our potential, step gingerly over our purpose, and stand apprehensively on the edge of our passion when we are comfortable cuddling with commonality.

There must be a day of reckoning that evokes the choice to answer the soul's beckoning to emerge from the shadows of someone else's perception of who we are and what we can accomplish.

The freedom to be ourselves is a divine birthright but the fear of rejection or disapproval drives us to compromise our individuality.

Success is often shackled by fear of the unknown, fear of being judged, fear of not being loved, and fear of our best never being good enough.

To be free of physical chains but living as a prisoner inside of your own body is anti-liberty.

Kristie guides you one sentence at a time on how to deliberately build a powerhouse mindset for decades to come by embracing impactful confidence keys to succeed daily. Now is your defining moment to inhale fortitude and exhale freedom to be a powerhouse leader.

THINK POWERFULLY, SPEAK PROFOUNDLY, and LIVE PASSIONATELY!

About the Author

Kristie Kennedy, The Image Confidence Expert, is a TEDx Audacious Leadership keynote speaker and Authentic Lifestyle author. As the owner of Queenfidence®Global Image Consulting she specializes in four areas of peak performance: mindset mastery, massive momentum, magnetic messaging, and potential maximization. Her bodacious belief is a testament that you can shift from mediocrity to magnificence one daring action step at a time.

www.queenfidence.com

www.ingramcontent.com/pod-product-compliance
Lightning Source LLC
Chambersburg PA
CBHW050909160426
43194CB00011B/2341